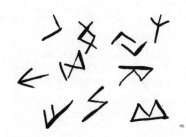

runes

KIM FARNELL

Previously published in 2006 as *Simply Runes* by
Zambezi Publishing Limited, Devon, UK

This edition first published in Great Britain in 2017 by
Orion
an imprint of the Orion Publishing Group Ltd
Carmelite House, 50 Victoria Embankment,
London, EC4Y 0DZ
An Hachette UK Company

1 3 5 7 9 10 8 6 4 2

Interior design by Kathryn Sky-Peck

A CIP catalogue record for this book is available
from the British Library.

Paperback ISBN: 978 1 4091 6951 2

eBook ISBN: 978 1 4091 6952 9

Printed and bound by CPI Group (UK), Ltd, Croydon, CR0 4YY

www.orionbooks.co.uk

Contents

The
Origins
of the Runes

It is believed that the runes originally were derived from a northern Etruscan alphabet, which originated among peoples who dwelt in northern Italy and who spread into south central Europe. The earliest forms of runic writing developed among people who were living in Bohemia. At some point, the idea of using symbols as a means of communication traveled northward along the river routes to the lands in northern Europe and Scandinavia.

Pre-runic symbols have been found in various Bronze Age rock carvings, mainly in Sweden, and some of these are easily identifiable in later alphabets. Rune figures can be found chiseled into rocks throughout areas that were inhabited by Germanic tribes. These people shared a common religion and culture and their mythology was passed on through an oral tradition. The people of northern Europe used the rune script well into the Middle Ages. In addition to a written alphabet, runes also served as a system of symbols used for magic and divination, so in this way the process of writing became a magical act.

The arrival of Christianity in any particular Nordic area often resulted in a decrease or complete cessation of belief in local mythologies. However, it was the Vikings who colonized Iceland, so Christianity had a much weaker influence in that region. The pre-Christian myths were first written down in Iceland as a means of preserving them. When the Roman alphabets became the preferred script of most of Europe between the thirteenth and sixteenth centuries, rune writing fell into disuse. Interest in the runes began to rise again in the seventeenth century, but the Christian church soon banned them. Runes have now been rediscovered as a symbolic system and have become very popular as an accurate means of divination. Their meanings derive partly from life in ancient times—for example, viewing cattle as a form of wealth—and partly from the stories of the Nordic gods and Norse mythology.

Runic History in Detail

It is clear that the runes have always performed two functions: (1) that of containing, conveying, and imparting information through inscribed symbols—as a form of writing—and (2) for purposes of divination and magic.

Before the Germanic peoples of Western Europe possessed a true alphabet, pictorial symbols were carved into stones. About 3,500 stone monuments in Europe, mainly concentrated in Sweden and Norway, are claimed to have been inscribed with runic types of pictures, symbols, and signs. The earliest of these writings date from about 1300 BC, and it is likely they were linked to sun and fertility cults. The names given to the runes indicate that a certain power was ascribed to them. The most famous users of the runes were the Vikings, who inscribed them everywhere they went.

The name *rune* means "a secret thing or a mystery." When the high chieftains and wise counselors of Anglo-Saxon England met, they called their secret deliberations "ruenes." When Bishop Wulfila translated the Bible into fourth century Gothic, he rendered St. Mark's "the mystery of the kingdom of God" and used the word *runa* to mean mystery.

When the Greek historian Herodotus traveled around the Black Sea, he encountered descendants of Scythian tribesmen, who crawled under blankets, smoked themselves into a stupor, and then cast marked sticks in the air and "read" them when they fell. These sticks were used as a kind of runic form of divination. By AD 100, the runes were already becoming widely known on the European continent.

The most explicit surviving description of how the runes were used comes from the Roman historian, Tacitus. Writing in AD 98 about practices prevalent among the Germanic tribes, he reports:

> To divination and casting of lots they pay attention beyond any other people. Their method of casting lots is a simple one: they cut a branch from a fruit-bearing tree and divide it into small pieces which they mark with certain distinctive signs (*notae*) and scatter at random onto a white cloth. Then, the priest of the community, if the lots are consulted publicly, or the father of the family, if it is done privately, after invoking the gods and with eyes raised to the heavens, picks up three pieces, one at a time, and interprets them according to the signs previously marked upon them. (Chapter 10, *Germania*)

Runes were used to foretell the future by casting, and they were also inscribed into tools, weapons, and many other items. Runic letters were also used by the clergy as an alternative to the Latin alphabet.

According to Norse belief, the runes were given to Odin, the father of creation, who was able to communicate with his people through the runes and gave them warnings, blessings, and even curses from their enemies.

The runic alphabet, known as the Futhark, appears to have been derived from two distinct sources. The first is considered to be Swedish, where pre-runic symbols have been found in various Bronze Age carvings, while a second case has been made for a Latin and Greek derivation of the runic alphabet. The roots of the runes are still argued among scholars. The strongest evidence appears to point toward a north Italic origin. There are close parallels between the forms of the letters used in that area, in addition to the variable direction of the writing. Both Latin and Italic scripts derive from the Etruscan alphabet, which explains why so many runes resemble Roman letters. This would place the creation of the Futhark some-time before the first century BC, when the Italic scripts were being absorbed and replaced by the Latin alphabet. Linguistic and pho-netic analysis points to an even earlier inception date, perhaps as far back as 200 BC. As time went on, runes became standardized throughout Europe, in some places the runes numbering as few as sixteen, in other areas as many as thirty-six; however, twenty-four runes formed the basic alphabet or Futhark. The Anglo-Saxons are credited with spreading the runes throughout Europe.

The Common Germanic Futhark remained in use among most of the Teutonic peoples until approximately the fifth cen-tury AD. It was at about this time that the first changes in the Futhark emerged on Frisian soil. The fifth and sixth centuries were a time of great change for the Frisian language, during which many vowels shifted in their sounds while new phonemes were added. This necessitated the expansion of the rune row, and in this first expansion four new runestaves were added to represent the new sounds in the Frisian language. The changes in the Frisian language also represented many of the changes that would be seen in Old English. Starting in the eighth century, more runestaves were added. It must be pointed out, though, that some of these staves are not proper runes, but rather pseudo-runes.

In the eighth century, the Old Norse language went through changes. Sounds shifted, some ceased to be used, and others were added. Old Norse speakers reduced the size of the rune row from twenty-four to sixteen. As some sounds stopped being used, the runes that represented them accordingly fell out of use. Similarly, the sounds of some runes were taken over by other runes, which resulted in the disappearance of those runes as well.

Though we speak of the Younger Futhark as if there is only one, in reality there were two different Norse Futharks: the Danish and the Norwegian-Swedish. As might be expected of a script that often uses a single stave to represent several different sounds, the sixteen-rune row Futhark apparently proved practical for writing. Eventually, a system of "pointed runes" developed, whereby a runestave that denoted several sounds would have a point or dot added to it in a particular place to differentiate between sounds. This appears to have started in Denmark and spread outward. Unlike the Anglo-Frisian rune row, the Younger Futhark did not fall completely out of use, so the runes were being used well into the Middle Ages—so much so that Iceland eventually banned their use.

From the ninth through to the twelfth centuries, the runes were carried to Anglo-Saxon England and to Iceland. Rune carvings have been found as far afield as Russia, Constantinople, the Orkney Islands, Greenland, and—some believe—North America.

Shaped by the tribal wisdom of northern Europe, the Viking runes soon emerged. With the onset of Christianity, the runes were associated with demonic forces. By AD 800 rune use began slowly to wane on account of persecution of their users.

The situation was different in England; runes were not actively suppressed by the Church. They fell out of use—even for inscription purposes—by the ninth century, at which time they were overtaken by the Latin script. However, they were still being used (albeit in a more limited fashion) in Scandinavia and Iceland.

In 1486, the book *Malleus Maleficarum* by Henricus Institoris (Heinrich Institoris Kraemer) and Jacobus Sprengerus (Johann Sprenger) set off the witch hunt that was to spread throughout all of Europe. This book was more or less a guide to witch hunting and specifically mentioned runes:

> Or even let us conceive that if they superstitiously employ natural things, as, for example, by writing down certain characters or unknown names of some kind, and that then they use these runes for restoring a person to health, or for inducing friendship, or with some useful end, and not at all for doing any damage or harm, in such cases, it may be granted, I say, that there is no express invocation of demons; nevertheless, it cannot be that these spells are employed without a tacit invocation, wherefore all such charms must be judged to be wholly unlawful.

Nevertheless, the runes did not disappear. The Elizabethan magician John Dee worked with runes, and mystical works about rune interpretation and magic continued to be written.

Calendars known as primstave, or runstaf, were used to mark Church holy days as well as planting and harvesting times, and persisted beyond the medieval period in Scandinavia. An indication of their enduring popularity is evident from a seventeenth-century inscription on a church choir wall in Oland, Sweden, which reads, "The pastor of the parish should know how to read runes and write them." Among the country people of Dalarna, a remote region of western Sweden, knowledge of the runes continued into the twentieth century. In Norway, among the Lapps of Finnmark in the country's far north, drums that have runes painted on them are still in use today by local shamans.

Until the seventeenth century, runes were in such common use that they were found on everything from coins to coffins. In some places their use was actually sanctioned by the Church. Even the common people knew simple runic spells, and runes were frequently consulted on matters of both public and private interest. However, in 1639, they were banned by the Church, along with many magical arts, in an effort to "drive the devil out of Europe." By this time, runes were of interest primarily to antiquarians, but during the Enlightenment, interest in the runes was rekindled. Scholars transcribed the runic poems and made the first studies into the runes and runic inscriptions. By the nineteenth century, many scholars were studying the runes.

In 1902, the Austrian journalist and author Guido Von List suffered a period of blindness following a cataract operation. It was during this period that he experienced a vision in which an alternative set of runes was revealed to him. He published the details of his experience in his book *The Secrets of the Runes*, in 1908. Von

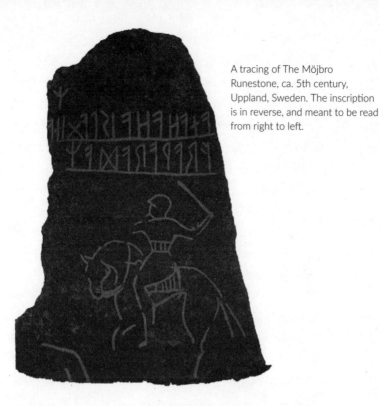

A tracing of The Möjbro Runestone, ca. 5th century, Uppland, Sweden. The inscription is in reverse, and meant to be read from right to left.

List was a German nationalist and his runes were linked with the mythological and racial ideology that was Armanism. He founded the Thule Society, which was an occult and right-wing political organization, in order to propagate his views.

In more recent history, the runes were revived by German researchers connected with the Nazi movement in the 1920s and 1930s. Although occultism was officially banned under the Nazis and many leading German occultists were imprisoned, key members of the party, such as Heinrich Himmler and Alfred Rosenberg, the official idealogue of the Nazi party, had a strong interest in the occult. Hitler was less interested, but he knew the value of symbols and incorporated Roman, Scandinavian, and ancient Germanic symbols of power into flags, staves, emblems, and uniform badges. The works of Von List therefore found favor, and his Armanen runes were adopted by the party for number of their badges and emblems. The Tiwaz (↑) rune served as the badge of the Hitler Youth movement. The rune Sowelo (ᛋ) (or *sigil* as it was known to the Nazis) was linked with the German word *sieg* (victory), and a doubled version of Sowelo became the logo of the SS. The lightning flash emblem of the British Union of Fascists was also inspired by this rune. During Nazi rule, runes were used throughout Germany—even on tombstones.

After the Second World War, most likely due to their association with Nazism, runes fell into disfavor, and very little was written about them until the 1950s and 1960s. Interest revived slowly as organizations such as the Odinic Rite and the Ring of Troth were formed to further the study of the northern mysteries and to pursue the religion known as Asatru.

It was not until the middle of the 1980s, with the widespread appeal of the "New Age" movement and the revival of pagan religions (especially the Asatru movement), that the runes regained their popularity as both a divinatory system and a tool for self-awareness. However, as early as 1937 runes gained ground in the United Kingdom with the publication of J. R. R. Tolkien's *The Hobbit*. Runes were used in the map and cover illustrations of the book. Tolkien continued to use runes as "dwarfish" writing in his other books. Runes appear on the title pages of *The Lord of the Rings*, which was published in 1954. Tolkien is said to have taken his runes from a Viking longboat discovered in the river

Thames. In the 1970s, heavy metal bands such as Led Zeppelin used runes as illustrations on album covers, and accusations of Satanism led to runes being associated with black magic during this period.

By the mid 1980s, a large number of rune books were being published. Ralph Blum's book, *The Book of Runes*, which was accompanied by a complimentary set of runes, started the trend, and it has continued to be the best seller in the genre. Blum drew very little upon the original lore. He even created his own order for the rune row rather than relying upon the traditional Futhark. Blum also introduced the blank rune, although he does not claim responsibility for inventing it. He claims it was included in a set of runes he purchased in Surrey. Many regard it as a misinterpretation of the runes, leading to an upset in their balance. Runes are now popular as a divinatory system, and many people in recent years have been attempting to reclaim their long history.

The Mythology of the Runes

All systems of divination stem from mythology, religions, philosophies, and beliefs. It is the instinctive fear of these so-called pagan ideas that leads those who sincerely believe in one of our modern religions to vilify these systems. Among those who learn the various divinations, some are fascinated by the stories that underpin them, while others view them as an irrelevance that gets in the way of their desire to use the particular system. However, without knowing what signs, symbols, and archetypes divinatory systems are derived from, how can anyone hope to understand their true meaning? The runes are so heavily dependent upon an ancient belief system, complete with a full cast of characters and a variety of occult meanings, that it is essential to have at least some understanding of the origins of their images.

The Believers

Hundreds of years before the Christian era, the Germanic people settled over much of Central Europe, living in what is now modern Scandinavia and Germany. Though covering a wide area, they shared a culture, and their myths were passed on through oral tradition. With the advent of Christianity, the northern and Teutonic mythologies faced an end to their development. However, when the Vikings colonized Iceland (which was less influenced by Christianity), their ancestral religion became preserved; thus, it is in Iceland where the myths were first recorded in writing. The tenth-century compilation *Eddas* offers thorough descriptions of cosmogony, mythology, and the traditions of the Teutonic and Nordic tribes. These early peoples were called Asatru, an Icelandic word meaning "those of the Aesir." Although replaced by Christianity, their religion was kept alive in Iceland and Lapland into the nineteenth century, and was revived in the 1970s. The Asatru worship the deities of the ancient Norse and Germanic peoples.

The Asatru believed in the "Nine Noble Virtues" of courage, honor, loyalty, hospitality, industriousness, truth, perseverance, self-discipline, and self-reliance. They revered their ancestors and their "honored dead"—those who were killed in battle—and they also revered nature and the spirits of the world. They held hospitality and truth as their highest ideals. The Asatru held four major holy celebrations, which occurred in autumn, at the beginning of winter, in midwinter, and at the beginning of spring.

The gods of Asatru were not seen as remote creatures but rather as beings who exerted an influence on the world and who were considered to be prone to the same flaws as humans. They were subject to the universal laws and could not escape Wyrd, the cosmic justice that forced them to face the consequences of their deeds. Death would come to them all at the end, particularly at Ragnarok—the Twilight of the Gods.

Words and Language

We do not have to go very far into history for spelling to be a moveable feast. For instance, in British English the following words are all spelled differently: *behaviour, travelling, centre, symbolise,* and *criticise.* The spelling associated with the runes and their history stretches across many centuries and languages, so there are many variations in the way these mythical characters and places are written within each type of Futhark. In this book, I have made my own choices and kept them reasonably consistent, although there are some extremely obvious slight variations. For instance, Muspell is sometimes referred to as Muspellheim—*heim* being "home or place of." Interestingly, *heim* still means "home or area" in modern German. In addition, there is no distinction between common and proper nouns in German, so all nouns are written with a capital letter, as are the words Futhark and Aettir in this book.

The Beliefs

At the beginning of time there was Muspell, which was the realm of Fire. Only the Fire Giants could tolerate the light and heat of Muspell. It was guarded by Sutr, who was armed with a flaming sword. It was believed that at the end of the world he and his companions would destroy the gods and that the world would be consumed by fire. Outside Muspell was an empty land called Ginnungap. To the north was a land of dark and cold called Nifelheim with eleven rivers that flowed from a great well, which froze and occupied Ginnungap. When the wind, ice, and cold met the heat of Muspell in the center of Ginnungap, a place of light, air, and warmth was born and thawing drops of ice appeared. The Frost Giant, Ymir, slept beneath the melting ice. Under his left arm grew a pair of male and female giants. One of the male's legs begot a son with the female. The melting frost became a cow, Audhumla, from whose udders ran four rivers of milk that fed Ymir. After a day spent licking ice, she freed a man's hair. After two days, she freed his head. And on the third day, she freed him completely. This man was called Bury. Bury married Bestla, the daughter of a giant, and they had three sons called Odin, Vili, and Ve'.

The three brothers killed Ymir and carried him to the middle of Ginnungap, creating the world Midgard from his body. Ymir's blood became the sea and lakes, and his skull became the cover of the sky. His brains became the clouds; his skeleton became the mountains; his teeth and jaw became rocks and pebbles; and his hair became the trees. The maggots from his flesh became dwarves, who looked like humans and had human understanding, and lived in the earth. The sparks and burning embers from Muspell gave light, and the stars were named and set in their paths.

Midgard was surrounded by an ocean. Odin, Vili, and Ve' gave lands to the friendly giants who were called the Etin. The Etin created a man and woman from two trees. Odin filled them with spirit and life, while Vili gave them understanding and movement, and Ve' gave them clothing and names. The man was named Ask (Ash) and the woman Embla (Elm), and they are the ancestors of all humans. The brothers then built Asgard, the home of the gods. Odin married Frigga, the daughter of the giant Fjirgvin.

The World Tree, Yggdrasil, rose from the center of Asgard, with its branches reaching over Asgard. One of its roots reaches into the underworld Hel (also called Hell or Helheim). Another root led to the world of the Frost Giants, and a third root led to the world of humans. Underneath the world tree is the Urda well, which was guarded by the Norns, the goddesses of fate who used the well to irrigate the roots of Yggdrasil.

The Norns were three sisters, goddesses of fate, who had some link with the older, pastoral gods called the Vanir. They represented time, so Urd, the Norn of the past, was depicted as an ancient crone who constantly looked back to the good old days. The young and lively Verdandi, Norn of the present, looked alert, while Skuld, the Norn of the future, was mistily pictured in a veil holding an unopened scroll. The Norns were occasionally led by an elemental force called Wyrd, who some scribes recorded as a person representing their mother. The Norns wove the Web of Wyrd (fate), which sets out the fate of gods and humans. This web was so huge that it covered the known world—it is interesting to note that the word *weird*, with its strange e-before-i spelling, still lingers in our consciousness today.

The wells of Hvregelmer and Mimir also fed Yggdrasil. The dragon Nidhog laid in Hvregelmer's well and gnawed on the roots of the tree. Mimir's well was the well of wisdom and was guarded by Mimir. Odin gave his right eye for a drink of the water from Mimir's well.

Mimir originally possessed the knowledge of the runes, which he obtained from the underground fountain that lay beneath the middle root of the World Tree that he guarded. After being pierced by a spear, Odin hung upside down from World Tree with no food or drink for nine days and nights. On the ninth night, he saw the shapes of the runes in the tree's roots. Crying out, he caught up the runes from the World Tree. Besla's brother gave him a drink from the fountain. He received nine of the songs that were the basis of the magic that lies in the application of the power of words and of the runes over spiritual and natural forces. The runes then became a channel for the protection of the gods, which enabled them to assist their worshippers when in danger or distress.

The runes of Victory could stop weapons and make those who Odin loved protected against the sword. Other runes had powers that controlled the elements, gave speech to the mute, freed the limbs from bonds, protected against witchcraft, took strength from the love potion prepared by another man's wife, helped in childbirth, healed the sick, gave wisdom and knowledge, and extinguished enmity. Odin taught the knowledge of the runes to his own clan; Dinn taught the elves; Dvalinn taught the dwarves; Asvinr taught the giants; and Heimdal taught the runes

Odin sacrifices himself by hanging from the World Tree, Yggdrasil. Illustration for "Hávamál," in *Den ældre Eddas Gudesange*, 1895 edition.

to humanity, in particular to selected noble families who were said to possess the power of the runes as a gift of the gods.

The gods built a bridge from a rainbow between Asgard and Midgard and rode across it daily. It was guarded by the god Heimdal, who supposedly slept lighter than a bird, could see one hundred travel-days in each direction, and could hear grass and wool grow. It is said that the bridge will collapse when the Frost Giants ride over it at Ragnarok.

The gods were divided into two groups: the Aesirs and the Vanir. The Vanir, or earth gods, symbolize riches, fertility, and fecundity, as they were associated with the earth and the sea. The most important gods of the Vanir were Njord, Freyr, Aegir, and Freya. The Aesir, or sky gods, symbolized power, wisdom, and war, and were not immortal. The Aesir lived in Asgard in two buildings, Gladsheim for the gods and Vingolf for the goddesses. The Vanir were the older race of gods and were also masters of magic. They lived in Vanaheim.

There was a clash between the two sets of gods, making the Aesirs, led by Odin and Frigga, and the Vanir, led by Heimdal, Freyr, and Freya, into enemies. The spark that ignited this war was an attempted murder by the Aesirs of the oracle and sorcerer Gullveig, who was said to be concerned only with her love for gold. The Aesirs burnt Gullveig to ashes three times, but each time she recovered. The Vanir, angered at her treatment by the Aesirs, prepared for war.

Eventually, peace was declared, and the gods exchanged hostages. The Vanir sent Njord and his children, Freya and Freyr, to Asgard, while the Aesirs sent Honir and Mimir to Vanaheim.

Honir caused the Vanir to be suspicious. Believing they had been cheated, they beheaded Honir and sent his head back to the Aesirs. The dispute was eventually resolved. The Vanir became assimilated, and all the gods continued to live in Asgard.

Odin was the leader of the gods. Thor was the god of thunder, and Loki was a giant who became an Aesir by adoption, thus a blood brother of Odin. Loki was a trickster. Odin's son, Baldur, settled disputes. Baldur had a dream in which his life was threatened. His mother, Frigga, forced the elements of fire, water, metal, and earth—as well as stones, birds, and animals—to swear not to harm him. Loki discovered that the only thing that could harm Baldur was mistletoe—so he created a set of arrows with it. He took the arrows to the blind god Hodor, who was Baldur's brother, and had Baldur killed. Baldur did not die in battle, so he was sent to Hel. Odin begged for Baldur's release. Hel, who was Loki's daughter, decided to release Baldur only if everything in the world, alive or dead, wept. The only one not to respond to Hel's plea was the giantess Thokk, who was actually Loki in disguise. The Aesir captured Loki and chained him beneath a serpent that dripped venom upon him as punishment for his crimes, causing him great pain.

The Future of the Gods—and of the World

When Mimir ceases to guard his well, Yggdrasil's root will start to rot, and the Nidhog dragon/serpent will gnaw through the root at Hvregelmer's well. Odin's sacrificed eye will see the coming of three years of an endless winter followed by Ragnarok. One of Yggdrasil's branches will break and fall, striking Jormungand (the world serpent), which immediately will let go of its tail. [Note: Some traditions suggest that Jormungand is a turtle and that the tree and the world are all perched on its back. The popular fantasy books by Terry Pratchett use this myth as their basis.]

The Het ship, Naglfar, will become visible in the mist. The wolves Skoll and Manegarm will move closer and closer to Sun and Moon. Loki will be released by giants, and Nidhog will leave the roots of Yggdrasil and head toward Asgard. As the giants march on Asgard, Heimdal will sound a warning and Loki will lead the monsters and giants in their last great battle. Many of the gods will die and the World Tree will fall down and burn. Some Aesir will escape in Frey's ship. Midgard will be destroyed by fire and sink back into the sea. Finally, the earth will re-emerge from the sea, and seven sons of the dead Aesir will return to Asgard and rule the universe.

The Nine Worlds

Before continuing, we need to fully understand the nine worlds that comprise the universe and which are all connected by the roots and branches of the World Tree, Yggdrasil, and which are subject to the web of Wyrd. Odin traveled freely through these worlds on the back of his mighty eight-legged stallion Sleipnir. Ancient sorcerers also traveled on dream journeys through these worlds using the runes as talismans, amulets, and keys to other realms of existence. Keep in mind the following:

- Midgard was the world of mortal humans—our world.

- To the north lay Nifelheim, the world of the dragon Nidhog.

- Jotunheim was the world of the Giants, which lay on the outer fringes of creation.

- Muspell lay to the south and was the world of fire.

- Vanaheim was the original world of the old Vanir gods.

- Alfheim was the world of the Elves.

- Swartalfheim was the world of the Dark Elves.

- Helheim was the lowest realm, the home of the dishonored dead—those who did not die in battle.

- Asgard was the highest realm and the home of the Aesir gods. It was also the location of Valhalla, the home of Odin and the honored dead—a kind of Nirvana.

Making Your Own Runes

1

When you make your own set of runes, you inject your own personal energy into them, and fill them with a power that will help you in your readings. A handmade set of runes is a sign of your dedication to the craft, and these will mean much more to you than a set purchased in a shop. Making a set of runes need not be difficult. You may also consider making a bag or box to keep them in. Natural fibers such as silk or linen are normally used for such bags, which can then be embroidered with one or more rune designs. The bag will need to be large enough to hold all your runes and to

allow your hand to slip into it in order to pull the runes out. You may choose to keep the bag inside a special box or inside a second bag made of a tougher material, such as leather.

Choosing Your Material

Runes have traditionally been made from a variety of materials, though many modern sets are made from wood. Anything robust and lasting is suitable as runes are bound to receive a lot of wear and tear. Each type of material has its unique energy and history.

You may wish to gather and use stones, cut small slices from a fallen tree branch, or use clay or some other material. Using stones will give you a durable and lasting set of runes but you will need to ensure that you have enough stones that are the same size and texture, because you shouldn't be able to tell which rune is which simply by touch. Wood can be cut, sanded and painted, but wood burns easily, holds water, and is difficult to clean, so it is important that you apply varnish to runes made of wood.

Stones

The stones themselves need not be special but you will want to gather them from a place that has meaning for you. They need to be as similar in weight and size as possible and they must be thoroughly washed. You can varnish the stones before painting a symbol on each or you could paint directly onto the stones with acrylic paints and then varnish with an acrylic sealer. Acrylic is water-soluble until dry, so it is easy to correct any mistakes you might make. The sealer will ensure that the paint doesn't chip when the runes rub together in your bag. If you choose a glossy varnish, this will make your runes look shiny.

Wood

Runic designs were first carved into wood, which is why the letters are formed from lines rather than bends, curves, or circles. To carve runes into wood, you must cut *across* the grain of the wood rather than going with the grain, which will make the designs appear to vanish into the wood's growth rings. One simple way to make wooden runes is to use oval discs bought from a craft shop. They are consistently sized.

Birch, yew, or fruit trees are often used for making runes. Fruit-bearing trees are more traditional, but you can choose any tree that appeals to you. Always make an offering to the tree before you cut into it and tell it why you want to take its wood. You might want to cut a branch bending to the north, or perhaps some other direction that appeals to you. Many people prefer to search for fallen branches rather than to cut into living wood, but ensure that the fallen wood you choose is not so dried out that the surface of the runes is likely to be rough. If you do cut into living wood, you will need to thank the tree for the gift that it has given you. The branch can then be cut into circular discs and the runes can then be marked by pencil, then painted, carved, engraved, inked, or burned into the wood. It takes about 30 inches of branch to make a full rune set (and to also have a few blanks for spares in case one or two get damaged later). Once you have cut or marked the runes onto the wood, you can add a decorative color or stain to the design. Each set made in this way will be unique, bearing the characteristics of a single branch from a single tree. A gloss finish is most attractive for the majority of woods, but ash, rowan, sycamore, and a few others look better with a matte surface.

Yew has a long history of association with the runes and with magic, but there are many other woods that have their own magical associations. Rune spells and talismans were traditionally cut or scratched into the type of wood that was appropriate for a specific type of spell or energy. The list below shows the types of tree and their associated gods and ideas.

Alder

This tree has an oily, water resistant wood and is used for making whistles. It is associated with one of the Giants who later became part of Welsh Celtic mythology as "Bran the Blest"; legend has it that Bran brought the cross to Britain. It is said that his head is buried under the White Tower at the Tower of London. This tree is said to be known for its strength in making amulets of protection and providing oracular powers.

Apple

This tree has a dense, fine-grained, rosy-colored wood with a slightly sweet smell. In Norse myth, Idunna was the keeper of the "apples of immortality," which kept the Gods young. It is associated with choice and is useful for love and healing.

Ash

This tree has a strong, straight-grained wood. The European variety was referred to in the *Eddas* as the species of Yggdrasil— the World Tree. Ash can be used in spells requiring focus and strength of purpose, and is associated with linking the inner and outer worlds.

Beech

This tree has a closely grained wood. Beech is associated with ancient knowledge as revealed in old objects, places, and writings. Beech indicates guidance from the past, and for the purpose of gaining the kind of insight that provides protection. Beech provides a solid base upon which all things rely.

Birch

The birch tree has a pale, fine-grained wood. It is associated with fertility and healing magic. Within living memory, criminals in

British prisons were actually "birched" (hit with a collection of birch sticks) as a punishment. One wonders whether the jailers who did this realized that they were following a pagan tradition that was designed to drive out the evil influences that had supposedly entered the criminal being thrashed! Birch was associated with Thor and it is a useful adjunct for fertility and healing spells.

Blackthorn

A winter tree, blackthorn has black bark and is covered with vicious thorns and it grows in dense thickets. The wood is used for making the cudgel and shillelagh. Its thorns were used to pierce waxen images. Blackthorn indicates the irresistible action of fate or outside influences that must be obeyed.

Elder

In Norse mythology, the goddess Freya chose the black elder for her home. In medieval times it was the abode of witches; it was considered dangerous to sleep under its branches or to cut it down. Elder indicates the end in the beginning, and the beginning in the end.

Elm

The elm tree has a slightly fibrous, tan-colored wood with a slight sheen. Elm is associated with the mother and earth goddesses and it said to be the abode of "faeries." Elm wood is valued for its resistance to splitting. The inner bark was used for cordage and chair caning. Elm adds stability and grounding to a spell.

Fir

Fir cones respond to rain by closing and to the sun by opening. Fir is said to be able to see over great distance to the far horizon beyond and below. It indicates high views and long sight with clear vision of what is beyond and yet to come.

Hawthorn

This tree has a light, hard, apple-like wood. The wood from the hawthorn provides the hottest fire known. In medieval Europe it was associated with witchcraft and considered to be unlucky. Hawthorn can be used for protection, love, and marriage spells.

Hazel

Hazel is commonly used for water divining. Magically, hazel wood is used to gain knowledge, wisdom, and poetic inspiration.

Holly

This tree has a beautiful white wood with an almost invisible grain. Holly is associated in both Pagan and Christian lore with the symbolism of the death of the land in winter and its rebirth in spring. Holly may be used in spells for sleep or rest and also to ease the passage of death.

Larch

This tree has a light, soft wood that is very similar to that of spruce. The smoke from burning larch is said to ward off evil spirits. Larch may be used for protection and to induce visions.

Maple

This tree has a very hard, pale, fine-grained wood. Maple can bring success and abundance.

Oak

This tree has a richly-colored dark brown wood. Oak has been considered sacred by just about every culture that has encountered the tree, although it was held in particular esteem by the Norse and Celts because of its size, longevity, and nutritious acorns. The oak is frequently associated with Thor. Oak can be used in spells for protection, strength, success, and stability.

Pine

This tree is an evergreen and it is associated with guilt or feelings of guilt.

Poplar

An Anglo-Saxon rune poem to refers to the poplar as being associated with the rune Berkano. The poplar is associated with the ability to resist and to shield, to endure and conquer. A further association links this tree with speech, language, and also with the winds.

Rowan (Mountain Ash)

The rowan tree is long known for its ability to protect against enchantment, and it indicates protection and control of the senses from enchantment, seduction, and beguilment.

Willow

The willow is a water-loving tree. In Western tradition it is a symbol of mourning and unlucky love. Willow indicates cycles, rhythms, and the ebb and flow of events and of life.

Yew

This tree has a smooth, gold-colored wood with a wavy grain. It has long been associated with magic, death, rebirth—and the runes. The yew is said be the oldest tree in the world, although this belief arose before the discovery of Australia and the much older forms of antipodean tree. There are convincing arguments for it being the original World Tree of Scandinavian mythology. Yew may be used to enhance magical and psychic abilities and to induce visions.

Bone

Another natural product that may be used for runes is horn or bone. Some people have been known to collect the bones after a barbecue for this purpose! If you want to use bones you need to boil them for several hours until all the meat and marrow are gone and they are bleached white. To cut the tiles you will need a hacksaw and blade that is capable of cutting through bone. After painting the symbols you will need to seal the bone so that the paint doesn't chip off. Bone can become very brittle, so it needs to be coated with varnish.

Clay

Traditional clay can be used to make runes but it will need to be fired, so it is only practical for those of you who are in contact with people who make and fire pottery. It is now possible, however, to buy clay that will harden through air drying, or that can be dried in a conventional oven. This type of clay is available in most craft and toy stores. You can form the clay into small balls and then flatten them slightly against a table. Then, use a sharp stick or a knife to incise the runes into the clay. When the clay has hardened, the incisions can be made to stand out by filling them in with ink or paint. You will need to varnish the finished clay runes. Clay is available in a variety of colors so it's easy to choose a color that reflects the nature of each rune.

Glass

The glass stones that are sold to be put into the bottom of fish tanks come in a variety of colors, and these can be painted with enamel paints.

Marking the Runes

Traditionally, blood would be used to mark a set of runes, so purists still choose a red medium, but it is not necessary to do so. Your choice of marking method will depend very much on the material from which you have chosen to fabricate your runes. If you are painting onto a flat surface, then acrylic or enamel paints will be suitable. You will need a good quality, fine paintbrush for your work. If you are using wood, you can purchase a wood-burning kit (available in craft and toy stores), and the runes can be burned into your wood slices. If you have incised your runes then you may want to rub a metallic paint into your incisions in order to highlight the script.

Consecrating your Runes

Once you have finished making your personal set of runes, you should consecrate them. Consecration is an act that implies making something special, and it also incorporates a principle of cleansing. The first stage of consecration is called smudging, which means exposing the runes to the smoke of herbs or incense. This stage takes the runes through air, representing the mind, and then smoke, representing the spirit. In the second stage of consecration, salt is sprinkled over the runes, which is symbolic of the earth. Rather than applying salt, some people bury their runes in the earth for a few days. The third stage of consecration is water, so some spring water should be poured into a clean dish and the runes submerged in it. The fourth stage of consecration is through fire. This can be done by swiftly passing each rune through the flame of a burning candle.

After the runes have been consecrated they can be activated for use. This can be done by placing each rune in the palm of your left hand, making a cylinder of your hand, and then blowing through it.

These runes are now unique to you alone, and other people should not use them without your express permission. While you are consecrating your runes, you may want to consider each rune and meditate on its meaning and also ask Odin, the supreme god in Norse mythology, to bless them for you.

Interpreting the Aettir

2

There are three Aettir (Aettir is the plural of Aett). One of the functions of each Aett is to act as part of an initiatory structure, each Aett being one degree in a three-degree initiation system. Initiation systems are a method of moving from one level of competence, knowledge, or skill to the next. The same idea exists in the study and application of magic, the kabbalah, freemasonry, religion, or any other system that has a recognized promotion ladder that is based on knowledge and skill.

The Aettir also reflect the ancient societal divisions of nurturer, warrior, and priest/king. The divisions are reflected in the Aettir of the runes in different ways. There is overlap in the duties of the runes and each Aett has its complement of functions and its own character.

Freya's Aett

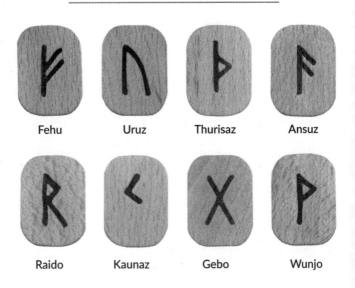

| Fehu | Uruz | Thurisaz | Ansuz |

| Raido | Kaunaz | Gebo | Wunjo |

Hagal's Aett

Hagalaz   Nauthiz   Isa   Jera

Eiwaz   Pertho   Algiz   Sowelo

Tyr's Aett

Tiwaz   Berkano   Ehwaz   Mannaz

Laguz   Inguz   Othila   Dagaz

Each Aett ends with a rune of positive nature and greater scope. Each Aett contains certain runes that cover similar concepts. For example each has a rune for light, as in Kanauz the torch, Sowelo the sun, and Dagaz the day. The light becomes greater in power as we progress through the Aettir. Similarly, each Aett also has a rune referring to wealth, as in Fehu, Nauthiz, and Othila. Each Aett has a different emphasis. Freya's Aett has four runes of danger, evil, or cost (Uruz, Thurisaz, Raido, and Gebo). Hagal's Aett has three (Nauthiz, Isa, and Pertho), and Tyr's Aett only one (Laguz, the dangerous sea). Each Aett has at least one rune of protection, one that is useful as a good luck charm, and one that is used in healing magic.

Each Aett has its own concerns. Freya's Aett is concerned with love, happiness, and enjoyment. Hagal's Aett is concerned with matters of achievement, power, and success, Tyr's Aett is concerned with justice, order, and spiritual advancement. The runes progress from personal and emotional concerns of love and pleasure, through worldly concerns of battle and achievement, to spiritual concerns of justice and godliness.

Some people choose to give different meanings to a rune that falls in a reversed position. However, not all of the runes can be read in the reversed position, so some rune users maintain that, although each rune may contain a negative form, its positive or negative energy is derived from its position among surrounding runes. In the following section the meanings are given for the negative form of each rune and I leave it up to you whether you chose to read reversed runes differently or not.

The Blank Rune

It is not traditional to use a blank rune although many commercially produced sets do include one. If you decide to include this in your set, you can consider its appearance as a kind of fated event, or something that is beyond the questioner's control for good or ill. The closest approximation to this is the Wheel of Fortune in the Tarot, which simply indicates that some kind of change is about to take place, but whether this is for good or ill depends upon the rest of the reading. In the case of the runes, a blank rune indicates a feeling is that fate, destiny, karma, or the uncontrollable force of Wyrd, the goddess of praise and punishment, is at hand.

Freya's Aett

3

Fehu, Uruz,

Thurisaz,

Ansuz, Raido,

Kaunuz,

Gebo, Wunjo

One

FEHU

The sound of "f"

Origin

The root meaning of the Fehu rune is "cattle." Cattle were an important aspect of the life of any agricultural community and they were vital to the economy. Therefore, this rune represents possessions won or earned and points achieved on the road to material gain. In an Anglo-Saxon runic poem, wealth is described as a "comfort to all men," and the poem goes on to say that it must be bestowed freely upon those who wish to gain favor. In an Icelandic rune poem, wealth is regarded as a source of discord. Generally linked to the Aesir, this rune is also often linked to Freya as it is first in Freya's Aett.

Positive interpretation

Fehu is concerned with wealth, material fulfillment and ownership, and in modern terms, this includes money. In general it represents happiness and prosperity but it also represents the kind of property that can be bought and sold. It indicates success in ventures since it represents not only the power to obtain wealth, but also the strength needed to hold on to it; thus Fehu is also a rune of power and control.

As the first rune in the set, one would suppose that it suggests a time of beginnings, of fresh starts, but in many ways it refers to the previous phase and cycles that have already been completed. Fehu shows that you have reached your goals, accomplished what you are trying to achieve, and that it is time to rest and enjoy the fruits of your labors. The loose ends have been tied up, you have gained abundance through your efforts, and you now have a kind of inheritance of well-deserved self-esteem, self-value, and success in ventures past. Furthermore, there is a hint of further success to come. Fehu announces the arrival of the things that you have worked for, and it also suggests that you will overcome future opposition. It advises you to stick with whatever plan you have underway, and also to conserve and hold on to what you have. Fehu is concerned with your physical and financial needs and the self-esteem that can be gained from meeting these. It speaks of enjoying good fortune through sharing it with others. In modern terms, Fehu represents earned income, so it relates to your career, status, and position in the world. When it appears in a casting it can indicate that prosperity is coming to you in some form, perhaps financially. The precise type of gain will be indicated by the runes that surround it. For example, if Fehu appears with Berkano, it shows gain as a result of a personal relationship.

The overall feeling that Fehu conveys is that a successful cycle has been completed and it is now time to take the next step.

Negative or reversed interpretation

When reversed or surrounded by negative runes, Fehu may indicate a lack of wealth and a period of financial difficulty. It may also be interpreted as greed or an exaggerated interest in material matters. Fehu can indicate loose ends and unfinished projects. Taken at its most negative, Fehu represents loss, or possibly an offer that should not be accepted. It is connected to poverty and also the kind of domination by others that leads to a loss of self-esteem. If not strongly negative it can indicate a delay or obstacle. Fehu may caution you to avoid wasting resources and to think carefully of the effect your actions will have in the future.

In some cases, a negative interpretation of Fehu can indicate problems related to conception, fertility, and pregnancy.

Magical uses

In magic, Fehu is used to attract wealth and to protect property, as well as to gain power over the environment. As an amulet, it can be used for protection and to increase your power.

Two

URUZ

The sound of "oo"

Origin

Uruz represents the aurochs, the once great wild cattle of northern Europe that could never be tamed and which are now extinct. Julius Caesar described these cattle in "De Bello Gallico" as slightly smaller in size than an elephant, and of the color and shape of a bull. Aurochs had extraordinary strength and speed and were exceptionally ferocious. They were seen as a symbol of great strength and speed as well as a symbol of man's prowess. It is believed that the bull was dedicated to Thor, so this rune is often associated with him. Hunting the aurochs provided a test of strength and initiative, so this is seen as a rune of achievement. Uruz is also often taken to represent Urd, who is the crone-like eldest of the three Norns.

Uruz is associated with the old gods—the Vanir. It represents the primal creative force, so it represents assertive action, a bid for liberty, or a contained force that is straining to be free. It can denote a protective force, especially in reference to your children or your territory. In general terms, Uruz represents a formative or protective force that can shape things to come.

Positive interpretation

Uruz is always concerned with some sort of beginning, the birth of something new, and the end of one cycle and the start of another. It represents challenges and everything concerning the unknown. This rune contains great creative power; it also represents free will and the ability to make decisions that can take you onward into new circumstances. It is a force for change and indicates that it is time to take action. Personal success could be at hand, and you need to be ready to accept the power that comes with it. Uruz is the rune of strength, good health, and sometimes also advancement in your career. When included in a casting it can show that your dream or wish is coming to pass. In some positions it can represent the male in a relationship. Uruz represents a strong, masculine energy force and assertiveness.

The appearance of Uruz suggests that you will soon notice an improvement in business and finances, although you have to work for these. Although new challenges are ahead, you will have the energy to work at them. It is primarily a rune of good fortune, exciting events, and success. Uruz represents energy, passion, vitality, fertility, and the unconscious. It is mostly concerned with the natural and instinctive sides of our nature. It also represents bravery, questing, initiation, challenge, untamed spirit, masculinity, stamina, independence, strength, and action. The outlook is particularly good for vitality and the return of health after a period of sickness.

Negative or reversed interpretation

In its negative form, Uruz represents brutality, harshness, hatred, and change for the worse. It can also indicate the possibility that your own power will be used against you. It can indicate an unwillingness to take chances or to approach the unknown. It symbolizes a lack of willpower and motivation. Uruz is also connected with male violence, callousness, and abuse. When interpreted negatively in a reading, Uruz can indicate that you have failed to take advantage of the moment, and that it may be your own low self-image that is holding you back. Because this rune also represents low vitality, it can occasionally be indicative of sexual problems for a man. Uruz can be seen as unlucky, and indicates that a lack of energy or motivation may be the reason that you are missing out on opportunities to improve your life or your circumstances.

Magical uses

In magic, Uruz is used to clear obstacles or change circumstances. As an amulet it can be used to galvanize the wearer into action or to increase sexual potency.

Three

THURISAZ

The sound of "th" as in "thin"

Origin

Although the precise meaning of this rune has been disputed, it is generally accepted as being unpleasant in nature. It is usually taken to mean "thorn" and it is associated with giants, trolls, and demons. When used in a sequence of three runes, it can alter the meanings of succeeding two runes. It is said to have been used to invoke demons from the underworld. The thorn element of this rune symbolizes a sharp and unpleasant thing to touch; it may also have sexual connotations.

Thurisaz is a rune of the force which can be used for defense or for destruction. Thorny bushes were once used to protect boundaries and castles, and to enclose criminals. Thor is the god that is said to protect sacred enclosures, so this rune is associated with him. It is also associated with the Thursar, who were giants in Norse mythology. These are primal forces, elemental in nature. Therefore, this is a rune of testing and challenge as well as protection and defense.

Positive interpretation

This rune represents chaos and transformation, the destruction that is needed to allow space for renewal. It is also connected with lust and the combination of pleasure and pain. It can be frightening due to its tendency to reveal our darkest and most destructive natures. But the truth is that we have to tear down the old to make room for the new, so this rune represents a type of catharsis from which new energy and insight may arise.

Thurisaz opens the door to the future. It shows the survival of difficulties and the need to do the right thing, to take the right action, and to resist oppression or opposition. At times it indicates a sudden change without warning. It is associated with stubbornness and perhaps the need to put one's own entrenched opinions aside and listen to advice. It is also a rune of protection, symbolizing passive resistance and the ability to attack without fighting, and thus it can outlast disorder and chaos. Being associated with boundaries and the kind of thorny hedges that are used to keep cattle from straying, it signifies that you should understand your limitations and calculate any risky ventures with care. Challenges will be fraught with danger and there is even a risk of injury, so care must be taken.

When in a positive combination, protection and luck are on your side. However Thurisaz falls in a casting, it indicates that an important decision is at hand, and this can be of such vital importance that it may change your life forever. Reflection, due consideration, and seeking out good advice is essential if you want to make the right decision. Although hardship may be present, there should also be wisdom, because this rune demands a sense of focus and deep introspection.

Negative or reversed interpretation

In its negative form, Thurisaz represents an unwillingness to listen to information and advice, and the kind of obstinacy that can lead to conflict. A cycle of good luck may come to an end, so this is not the time to boast or to be too self-assured. You may encounter opposition from those who are stronger than you. Thurisaz warns us to be cautious in making decisions and to slow down, check out possibilities and options, and see what can be done. In short, if you proceed now, you must do so with immense caution. However, if you are unsure of the outcome of a specific decision or action, perhaps it is best to do nothing for the time being.

Magical uses

In magic, Thurisaz is used for protection and defense, or for those occasions when one needs to strike back at others. As an amulet it can be worn for protection.

Four

ANSUZ

The sound of "ah"

Origin

This rune has the meaning of "god" or "deity"—indicating specifically one of the Aesir. It is usually ascribed to Odin. It is related to the story of Odin and the way that he obtained the knowledge of the runes, so Ansuz is associated with the source of all language. It is also considered to be a blessing, joy, and comfort for the wise. As the worldly counterpart of the World Tree Yggdrasil, the ash tree is associated with this rune and this reinforces the connection with Odin.

This is the rune of inspired speech and incantation as a form of creative expression. It is linked with the passing of knowledge through the spoken word, and by extension it is also considered to be the rune of the poet. It represents the acquisition of inspiration and understanding. Ansuz is also associated with enthusiasm, manipulation, encouragement, and compassion. As the rune of the gods, Ansuz is very powerful; it represents divine powers and the intervention of the gods. It denotes all forms of direct communication, such as speaking and singing, and suggests that a combination of these can lead to divine inspiration, spiritual insight, and wisdom.

Positive interpretation

Ansuz symbolizes honesty, inspiration, and the good use of words. It also advises you to listen to your own inner voice. All matters related to communication are covered by this rune, including news, study, and teaching. Ansuz represents wisdom, sometimes the kind that emanates from the most unlikely source. It is the rune of intellectual activities and also of stability and order. As it represents the spoken word and communication, Ansuz is associated with taking advice and acquiring wisdom. In a reading, it often represents an intelligent individual who is full of energy. It can symbolize someone wiser (and perhaps older) than yourself who is able to offer good advice. Sometimes Ansuz suggests an apprenticeship under the guidance of someone who is able to teach you a great deal. It can also indicate a verbal test such as an oral exam or a job interview, and in this circumstance Ansuz will show that you can get through the test with ease. It indicates that knowledge may come from the most unexpected of sources and it also suggests that a little positive trickery can be helpful in current circumstances. Sometimes Ansuz shows that whatever has been holding you back will soon remove itself.

Negative or reversed interpretation

In its negative form, Ansuz indicates dishonesty, lies, trickery, and a refusal to learn the lessons of life. It shows loss and misunderstanding as well as betrayal. Others may interfere with your plans, or there could be a breakdown in communication. The advice you receive from others could be biased, thus it would be a good idea to seek a second opinion. Things are unclear and knowledge may be misused in some way. Sometimes it indicates an elderly person who is causing problems. In practical terms, Ansuz denotes a phase when correspondence goes missing, communications become fouled up, and journeys—that should be straightforward—turn into nightmares.

Magical uses

In magic, Ansuz is used to bring calm and help in making wise decisions, and also as a general aid in divination. As an amulet it can be worn to increase communication skills.

Five

RAIDO

The sound of "r"

Origin

A variety of meanings have been ascribed to this rune, including a journey, a cartwheel, a ride, and a cart. It is often associated with Thor who rode in a wheeled chariot, and thus also to thunder, which tradition tells us was caused when Thor drove his chariot across the sky. It is also associated with the god Foresti, the god of justice and son of Baldur.

Usually Raido is associated with wagons, which makes it the rune of the traveler, and it can offer protection to the traveler. Raido also signifies the passage of the sun and stars through the heavens, so it is also associated with spiritual and mental journeys. It can indicate that there is a path to follow that can solve a particular problem.

Positive interpretation

Raido refers to travel and also the means of transportation. It may signify a journey that is taken by necessity or one that is taken for pleasure, and if this is a literal journey, it will be safe, pleasant, and enjoyable. However, Raido can show a metaphorical pathway or road that can provide a way through a dilemma, a journey in consciousness, or a change of view. It represents the "vehicle" or method by which you achieve an objective or goal. It allows you to channel your energies effectively so that they will help you. Thus, the journey in question may be a journey of the soul, undertaken in order to bring about some form of healing. Representing movement and motion, Raido symbolizes travel and exploration but it can also denote a new start, taking control, leadership, and promotions. This rune suggests that now is a good time for negotiations and discussions, a time when it is possible to reach a compromise. Depending on the surrounding runes, Raido may indicate unexpected news or that now is a good time to buy or sell something of importance. In modern terms, this might be a vehicle, a computer, fax, phone, or some other form of communications equipment. Raido can refer to a quest and your destiny in following such a quest. Decisions need to be made with an ability to see the larger picture, as Raido advises not to focus solely on your problems or become isolated from daily events, but to take the wider view.

Negative or reversed interpretation

In its negative form, Raido suggests that now is a bad time for travelling, despite the fact you may need to do so. Delays, accidents, breakdowns, and problems are likely in any journey that you must take. Plans are likely to be upset, so it is best to postpone your journey for the time being if at all possible. Raido can indicate an unexpected and unplanned journey. Sometimes this refers to a course of action that is best left alone for the time being. Negotiations are unlikely to turn out well at this time and you may have to be extra patient with people. It is best to avoid legal or official dealings for the time being. It may signify a lack of goals and stagnation in your life, and the need to stop, think, and see what lessons need to be learned.

Magical uses

In magic, Raido is used to help you when searching the unknown and to help you to take control. As an amulet it can be worn to ensure a safe journey and to aid you in legal matters.

Six

KAUNAZ

The sound of "k"

Origin

A variety of meanings have been attributed to this rune, including a torch or light, a boil, abscess, and an ulcer. The most common attribution is "torch," although several sources do associate it with some form of discomfort or disease. It is also associated with cremation. Kaunaz represents internal fire on all levels, including that of inflammation and fever. This is the flame of the forge and deep earth energies, so it has an association with the dwarves who dwell in the deep earth. It is the flame of the artist and craftsman and, therefore, a force for creation. There is a close association with knowledge that is derived from such inspiration. At times Kaunaz represents the fire of a sexual relationship or the barrier that needs to be crossed in order to reach inner knowledge.

Positive interpretation

Primarily, Kaunaz is concerned with illumination and also the destruction that needs to take place to make way for the new.

It is concerned with dangerous forces that are hard to control. Although these forces are needed for our survival, they can also easily harm us. Kaunaz denotes insight, learning and knowledge, wisdom and enlightenment. When you are in the dark this rune can offer an opportunity to realize your highest potential. It can lead to new beginnings, but it can also represent the light of guidance and learning, because the light that it shines brings clarity and revelation.

Kaunaz is a rune of spiritual as well as intellectual enlightenment. It may also indicate good health and a positive attitude. If your life has been stagnating, this rune can show a change for the better. It is a good rune to find if you are undertaking any creative activity. Kaunaz suggests that the solution to your problems will be forthcoming; also that this is a time for seriousness and concentration. Sometimes Kaunaz represents a form of intellectual passion, but it can also occasionally denote physical and sexual passion. Whatever the scene, Kaunaz brings heightened emotions.

Negative or reversed interpretation

In its negative form, Kaunaz depicts a darkening of the light and perhaps a missed opportunity. It signifies the disillusionment and false hope. It can represent an ending or loss, and sometimes also poor judgment. Often it shows up when a relationship is coming to an end and the two people involved need to go their

separate ways. The lack of clarity associated with this rune leads
to confusion.

Magical uses

In magic, Kaunaz is used to restore self-confidence and strengthen
willpower. As an amulet it can be worn to enhance your insight.

Seven

GEBO

The sound of hard "g"

Origin

This rune means "gift," although the nature of the gift remains ambiguous. It is unclear whether Gebo refers to the sacrifice of humanity to the gods or the bounty of the gods to man. It is often translated to mean generosity. Gebo is often associated with Odin or Freya. As the gift rune, Gebo is concerned with mutual and unselfish giving. It represents the ability to sacrifice without expecting anything in return. Gebo also symbolizes the connection between the gods and men. It is the gift that brings connections through exchange, and it signifies the unity and honor created when an exchange takes place.

Positive interpretation

Gebo represents hospitality, generosity and giving. It is the point where the giver joins the one who receives. It has been related to the gift of wisdom received by the hero from the Valkyries. Gebo is a symbol of exchanged vows, marriage, and ecstasy, and it also represents the sacrifice of independence due to partnership, but also the increase due to consolidation. Joint efforts, partnership, love, and growth are represented by this rune. It is associated with all matters related to sharing and sacrifice. Often it will signify a new romance or an important development in a romantic relationship because Gebo suggests commitment. The gift it represents may be one of love, or a material one that comes along just when you need it. Gebo is the gift that binds a partnership. In modern times, it is common for us to sign the letters and cards that we send to our loved ones with an "X," but how many of us realize that we are actually using the Gebo rune for this purpose? Gebo usually indicates a time in your life that is full of peace and contentment.

Gebo can refer to an unexpected gain and benefits that arise from a joint effort. The relationship it refers to may be the one we have with our higher selves, and the sense of unity with all that surrounds us. Generally thought of as being lucky, Gebo shows the creation of harmony within relationships and the ability to balance opposing forces.

Negative or reversed interpretation

Although Gebo cannot be read in a reversed position, depending on the surrounding runes it may still have a negative form. It can indicate dishonesty, a lack of balance, or problems that are rooted in your emotions. Another thing to bear in mind is that if you are too ready to give to others, they may become dependent on your generosity rather than standing on their own feet. Also, if you stop giving or if you don't give enough in a particular situation, you may be seen as a miser.

Magical uses

In magic, Gebo is used to promote harmony and bring about union as well as to receive divine instruction. As an amulet it may be worn to bring harmony into your romantic life.

Eight

WUNJO

The sound of "v" or "w"

Origin

This rune means bliss, comfort, and glory; it primarily represents an absence of suffering. It is also associated with intoxication. Wunjo is one of the two runes that represent joy (the other being Sowelo). Wunjo represents physical and sensual energy and it carries a sense of playfulness with it. It is connected to the god Freyr due to its meaning of peace and joy. Love and falling in love are typical aspects of this rune. It is very much concerned with living in the present and indicates a condition of physical and emotional well-being.

Positive interpretation

Wunjo is associated with happiness and joy and the battle that is well-fought and won. It offers prosperity and friendship. Because it is associated with the wind, Wunjo can also be the means by which you alter the direction of something or change one situation into another; it can indicate that you are "running against the wind." It represents a state of harmony in a chaotic world and it provides a balance between all things. It shows the meeting point between opposites and the point at which alienation disappears. This is a rune of shared aims and it can mean that good news will come from afar.

Often Wunjo indicates luck, happiness, and success coming into your life. It may show deep affection and lasting emotional happiness. If may represent a person in a reading, especially if this person is the object of your affections. Sometimes Wunjo indicates a firm friendship rather than love. In general it represents pleasure and bliss, peace and serenity, along with a sense of fulfillment and harmony, and of hopes and wishes coming true. It rules the virtue of cheerfulness and suggests that you are able to keep any pain and sorrow from looming too large in your life. Wunjo indicates recognition of your achievements and the reward for your efforts. It can offer relief after a time of strife and it indicates that life is making a turn for the better. Sometimes this rune indicates good news from afar and also the return of health after a period of sickness, especially if there is someone around who helps you get back on your feet.

Negative or reversed interpretation

In its negative form, Wunjo represents impractical enthusiasm and unrealistic expectations, and it suggests unhappiness and sadness. Matters involving trust are at issue now; it may be that a loved one or business partner you trust or rely upon is turning out to be untrustworthy. At times Wunjo can show failure and loneliness. It may describe dissatisfaction with your job or performance. It suggests that you need to be cautious, and perhaps put off important decisions. Trouble may be coming from people who oppose you, but this will soon pass. Tradition says that you should delay decisions of a personal nature for at least three months, or of a business nature for at least three days.

Magical uses

In magic, Wunjo is used to bring happiness and success. As an amulet it can be worn to bring success to all your endeavors.

Hagal's Aett

4

Hagalaz, Nauthiz,

Isa, Jera, Eihwaz,

Pertho, Algiz, Sowelo

Nine

HAGALAZ

The sound of "h"

Origin

The meaning of this rune is "hail." Hagalaz recognizes the potential for destruction, and represents qualities of transformation. It is as though a period of frost and snow is required in order to break up and refresh the earth so that it can bring forth new fertility and growth. Representing primal chaos, Hagalaz is associated with Ymir. Out of this chaos comes a tangible force, which means that this rune signifies a dramatic event or disruption to one's life that comes from outside, and possibly from a completely unexpected source. A hailstorm can be devastating and it can ruin everything that lies in its path. Hagalaz is one of three runes associated with winter, which, to people living in the ancient Norse lands of Sweden and Norway, means a period of bad weather, wind, snow, ice, and restriction. The Norse were great travelers, so a bad winter made travel difficult, if not downright impossible. In time all things can transform from something bad to something good. This is a rune of the unconscious mind and the thought process. Hagalaz represents the basis for the laws that shape events in our lives, which suggests that the force it represents is not completely under our control.

Hagalaz can foretell a time of utter destruction of all that is familiar to you—the kind of major event that occurs in every life once in a while. Such a scenario might be a death in the family, divorce, sickness, sudden financial loss, or some other form of major setback. Sometimes it is merely a longed-for journey that has to be set aside. Fate is not with you at this time and life is hard; indeed, in some cases quite terrifying for a while.

Positive interpretation

Hagalaz is not simply destructive, but offers opportunity for great change and perhaps a journey from one world or lifestyle to another. It represents forces that cannot be avoided. As the rune of unexpected disruptions, it also signifies limitations and delays. The forces at work here are outside your control, and it may only be later you that you will see a reason for the limitations that are being imposed on you or the risks that you are being forced to take. Hagalaz refers to a time of testing, trial, penance, loss, pain, and suffering. Hagalaz demands that you let go of the past so that you have room for growth, acceptance, and fortitude. Its influence is disruptive, but it allows you the freedom to break out of your current cycle. Even if you are afraid of change or refuse to leave the past behind, Hagalaz will force you to break out. This is not a time for long-term plans since they are likely to be unsuccessful. Eventual success can be obtained but only after much effort on your part. When you look back on this time, it will stick in your mind as a period when your character was forged, when you developed a backbone, and achieved or lived through more than you thought possible.

You may feel that your future is in the hands of another person and this may be someone who you are not particularly familiar with. The advice of this rune is not to start anything new right now. It can sometimes refer to an interruption rather than complete destruction. Oddly enough, because of its connection with risk, this is a rune of gamblers and gambling.

Negative or reversed interpretation

Hagalaz cannot be read reversed, but in its negative form shows chaos and disruption, loss, and the need for shelter. It refers to unresolved matters, blaming others for shortcomings, and nostalgia for what has gone before. This may indicate accidents that are caused by rash behavior or by moving too fast. This is not a time for taking a risk or a gamble, so stop and think before taking any important steps.

Magical uses

In magic, Hagalaz is used to remove unwanted influences and to break destructive patterns. As an amulet it can be worn to protect against external aggression.

Ten

NAUTHIZ

The sound of "n"

Origin

Nauthiz is another of the shaping powers that form the fates of the world and humanity. It is associated with the Nornir who are the shapers. Nauthiz means "need" and this is a rune that represents the desire that drives us to obtain that which we want. It is strongly associated with sexual desire in addition to the desire to obtain or achieve. When directed, it can be creative and procreative, but when misused can be a force for destruction.

Positive interpretation

This rune has a meaning that vacillates between assistance and the need to survive. Working hard and making an effort will offer a solution to your difficulties at this time, although Nauthiz can signal hardships and great challenges. Nauthiz encourages you to concentrate on what is essential and on those things that really need to be done rather than to procrastinate or concern yourself with inessentials. It may be interpreted as a power source or perhaps as poverty and desperate need. Often it foretells hard work and a period of endurance. Necessity places constraints on you, so your possibilities are restricted, but Nauthiz also brings the power and strength to break free from restriction. Often this rune stands for delays and a need to exercise patience. It shows a time when you are passing through a difficult learning situation and a time when you are forced to face your fears. It is a time to avoid greed and to conserve your energy. Your emotional needs are unlikely to be met at this time. It is just possible that your problems are a result of blowing a situation up out of proportion.

Hardship, responsibility, and discontent are symbolized by Nauthiz, along with the frustration that these lead to. This rune represents the desire for what you fancy or what you think you deserve versus real needs, and the endurance and patience that are needed to gain your desires. Nauthiz frequently indicates that you find yourself coming into contact with some part of yourself that you do not like. It shows a time to appreciate what you have rather than longing for impossibilities, and this is a time during which to draw on your inner resources and strengths.

Assistance will come from older relatives and friends who stand by you through some very dark times. Determination and self-reliance can lead to change, but either way, this rune suggests that your luck will change for the better in the near future.

Negative or reversed interpretation

In its negative form, Nauthiz tells of a time of testing when your patience and sanity are pushed to their limits. It advises you to avoid making hasty judgments or setting off on the wrong path, so it is important to realize your mistakes and to be honest with yourself. You may have to right wrongs you have done to others in the past. The advice here is to avoid get-rich-quick schemes or quick-fix solutions, but just to stick to your path and wait for your luck to change.

Magical uses

In magic, Nauthiz is used to channel the kinetic energy that is tied up in sexual frustration and to give strength in times of need. As an amulet it can be worn to give inner strength in times of hardship.

Eleven

ISA

The sound of "ee"

Origin

Isa means "ice." Isa is an elemental rune that is associated with the Rind who refused Odin the means to avenge the death of his son. It is also associated with the Frost Giants who are called the Thursur. As frozen water, ice is considered to be static, and can therefore bring things to a halt. It may also be an expansive force, or one that crushes anything caught in its grasp. It may provide a bridge over dark water or a dangerous trap. Being self-contained, it has the power of control and constraint.

Spontaneity and activity have no connection to Isa; it emphasizes withdrawal and a time of standing still. There is an element of discipline contained in this rune, enabling it to act as a very powerful force. It warns us to avoid any tendency to exaggerated formalism or inhibiting strictness. Monotony results from its more negative manifestation. It is an effective protection against vulnerability and it can hinder emotional involvement. Isa tends to halt activity and delay progress.

Positive interpretation

When Isa is drawn it indicates a time of standstill and a freeze in a situation, so all plans should be put on hold. It often indicates temporary delays and frustrations and it may also indicate a relationship that is cooling off. Bad feelings and resentments are possible, along with problems relating to loyalty. Where love relationships are concerned, Isa indicates a really painful time when you need to accept that your lover is losing interest and that you may have to cut your losses and move on.

In one sense, the feeling of being frozen or in limbo can be a problem, but in another it also allows time for thought and a review of your situation. A sense of detachment comes about that enables you to focus your thoughts before moving onto a new stage. Reflection and withdrawal allow a time of rest and recuperation. It is time to shed outdated ideas so that you can unfreeze yourself from past patterns of behavior and to allow a thaw to follow. Just as spring follows winter, you will shortly turn the corner.

Negative or reversed interpretation

Isa cannot be read in a reversed position, but in its negative form it shows cooling relationships, deceptive beauty, restrictions, and delay. It shows the dangers of the path you are treading and the fact that you really do have to leave a no-win situation behind and move in a new direction.

Magical uses

In magic, Isa is used to strengthen powers of concentration and stabilize the personality. It is not usually worn as an amulet.

Twelve

JERA

The sound of "y" as in "year"

Origin

The meanings attributed to Jera include "year," "spear," and "harvest." It is connected with the completion of a cycle, the end of a season, or the close of a year, so Jera represents the rotation and change of the cycles. It can represent fruitful completion or the eternal contrast of opposites that provide a whole. Jera can bring peace and harmony and it states that what was sown can be reaped.

The whole cycle of life is contained within this rune of seed, growth, and harvest. Jera represents the meeting between the seasons, between light and darkness, day and night, man and woman. It signifies the sacred marriage ritual between god and goddess. Its association with sex as a means of survival as well as enjoyment leads to Jera's association with Freya. It also represents hopes and expectations for the future.

Positive interpretation

The lesson that Jera offers is that if we want to achieve great results, we cannot go against the natural order of things; we need to go with the flow. Events and changes will come at the proper time and we must take note of opportunities for new beginnings. This rune is concerned with reaping what you have sown and receiving rewards for your efforts, so it can indicate the end of a long project and a feeling of relief.

Jera can refer to intervention by a third party, such as when one engages the services of a professional person, and sometimes this indicates legal matters. It can also refer to buying a new home. Although the world may appear stagnant at the time of the reading, and things are going more slowly than you would like, there will soon be movement in your affairs and you will be able to harvest the seeds you have planted. Things will happen in their own space and time. What you have put out into the world will come back to you. Jera often refers to the repayment of money and favors. Delays may sometimes occur with legal or financial issues because Jera acts as a reminder that these things take time. Jera promises a beneficial outcome that will come in its own time, so patience is essential. It warns against judging others harshly because you may soon be judged yourself.

Negative or reversed interpretation

This rune cannot be read in a reversed position, but in its negative form indicates that problems can be overcome with a little careful effort. It also indicates that legal help may be needed. You may be called to account to pay for your past misdeeds, or you may be following a path to which you are not suited.

Magical uses

In magic, Jera is used to bring about change and also to bring your will into effect slowly and naturally. As an amulet it can be worn to help manifest your inner vision into physical reality.

Thirteen

EIHWAZ

The sound of "e" as in "eye"

Origin

Eihwaz means "yew," which is a tree that is sacred to runecraft and to the making of bows. The bow is associated with the hunting god, Ull. The yew also represents the World Tree, Yggdrasil, that Odin hung in until he obtained knowledge. The yew is said to contain the mystery of life and death, as its roots were thought to reach into the underworld.

Eihwaz is a rune of wisdom and provides protection by helping to increase personal power and the ability to defend yourself. It is a powerful symbol of protection and also of banishing. Yew is both strong and flexible and these concepts are encompassed in Eihwaz. As the yew gives freely of its fruit, this rune also represents patient and unselfish giving. However, the fruit of the yew is poisonous, which strengthens its association with death. Eihwaz possesses the power of both death and regeneration, and a regrowth from an old situation into the new.

Its position as the thirteenth rune means that Eihwaz is often considered as the death rune, although many scholars consider that the association of "unlucky 13" with Norse mythology is apocryphal. Prior to Christianity, thirteen was a lucky number that represented the thirteen lunar months of the year. The origin of "unlucky 13" appears to come from Christian sources, being attached to the thirteen diners at the last supper, and also in association with the fatal sentencing of the Knights Templar on Friday the 13th October, 1307. It may be that this latter event was where the "unlucky" association was first made, and that it was only later connected to the last supper and other biblical sources. (Hindu culture considers 13 an unlucky number, and in the West the association appears to have been relatively recent.) The yew tree is also associated with death in Christian culture due to the fact that it is frequently planted in cemeteries. Yew was believed to trap the souls of the dead; also, its roots reach into the realms of the dead and its branches into the realms of the living. Yew trees can live for centuries, so it may represent the of continuity of time.

Positive interpretation

Eihwaz symbolizes strength, reliability, dependability, and trustworthiness. It represents doing the right things and persevering until you have got them right. It is associated with the endurance and patience necessary to achieve the change in consciousness that allows for a spiritual rebirth. As a rune of protection and of hunting, Eihwaz shows that you have your sights on a reasonable target and that you can achieve your goals. Although minor delays and obstacles are possible, they are unlikely to cause too much trouble. As long as you are flexible and able to work with change you can turn any situation to your advantage. Think of the image of a bow being pulled back, readying itself for action. Eihwaz represents a time when you clear the decks and make ready for some new activity.

Often Eihwaz shows a tie to the past. When it appears in a reading, you may hear from someone from your past, and there is a possibility that things that were not dealt with previously can be successfully resolved now. It signifies a turning point in your life and, as long as you can put up with temporary discomfort, it brings good results.

Negative or reversed interpretation

Eihwaz cannot be read in a reversed position, but in its negative form it refers to the resurgence of an old problem that has not been properly dealt with. It also shows false nostalgia for the past and a sense of loss and confusion.

Magical uses

In magic, Eihwaz is used to bring profound change and to overcome difficulties, especially when you are looking for a new avenue. As an amulet it can be worn to protect you from your own weaknesses by rendering you sensible and thoughtful.

Fourteen

PERTHO

The sound of "p"

Origin

A variety of meanings have been associated with Pertho ranging from "dance" to "fruit-tree" to "hearth." It is also associated with the magical powers of the earth through an association with the Latin word *petra*, meaning rock. Additionally, Pertho is associated with the vulva and so bears an association with Freya, the mother of the gods and a symbol of female sexuality and birth.

Pertho's primary meaning is that of initiation, of things that are hidden and unexplained, and of the working of the fates, which leads to its association with the Nornir. It points toward that which is beyond our powers. Powerful forces of change are indicated, so at times it represents surprises, gains, or rewards that you did not anticipate. Associated with the deepest part of our being, Pertho is the bedrock upon which our destiny is founded. It can refer to transition or letting go of everything. Those things that you know on an unconscious level can come into the light and help you understand the higher meaning of things. Pertho suggests the vagaries of chance that cannot be controlled. It symbolizes the warrior who constantly tests himself against chance and luck. Pertho represents luck in action or any gamble or risk that is undertaken. It represents the uncertainties of life and the interaction between your personal free will and the constraints of your circumstances.

Positive interpretation

Pertho is the rune of memory, recollection, and problem solving. It indicates an unexpected resolution to difficult situations. As a rune of mystery, it reveals hidden things and secret or occult abilities. Its appearance often refers to the disclosure of some sort of secret. In general terms, Pertho refers to mysteries, the occult, psychic abilities, and revelation. Tradition says that if this is the first rune to appear in a casting, the reading should be aborted because any advice that follows will change the course of fate and anger the Norns.

Negative or reversed interpretation

In its negative form, Pertho may represent skeletons in the closet that are about to be revealed; those things from your past that you would prefer to keep hidden that come back to haunt you. Pertho refers to disappointments and letdowns. An unpleasant surprise could be ahead of you and obstacles are likely to appear and confound all that you are trying to do. It is best to accept the passing of old patterns and concerns from your life. This is no time to take risks.

Magical uses

In magic, Pertho is used to increase power and help gain wisdom. As an amulet it can be worn as an aid in childbirth.

Fifteen

ALGIZ

The sound of "z"

Origin

Algiz implies defense and protection, and has also been equated with the elk. It is a sign used to promote victory and protection as well as to strengthen magical power and luck. It is often associated with the Valkyries as a protective force. It is also connected to the animal kingdom and our contact with animal forces. In ancient Scandinavian magic the "fearhelmet" was considered a symbol of protection. This is made from four Algiz runes engraved on four sides of the helmet and meeting in the middle, thus creating a helmet that symbolically protects the wearer from his worst fears.

Positive interpretation

As a rune of protection, Algiz often tells of a fortunate new influence entering your life. It also suggests that this is the right time to follow your instincts. Friendships are in the forefront of your life now, and an old or new friend may offer assistance. Algiz may tell of an opportunity that someone will offer you; accepting the opportunity or offer can turn you in a beneficial new direction. Algiz may indicate that a guardian angel is hovering in the background. Algiz indicates assistance and warns of danger, in addition to indicating those people and places that will give you support. It offers new opportunities and challenges, along with the emotional stability needed to cope with them. Things may be turbulent at this time but Algiz indicates that you are making progress.

Algiz symbolizes resistant power and is the most powerful defense rune. It acts as a shield that can repel evil. If you are sick, this rune indicates the return of good health, and it can also signify friends and loved ones who help you to regain your health and strength. There is a slight warning for you to look after yourself and not to wear yourself out on behalf of others or to allow lame ducks to drain you.

Negative or reversed interpretation

In its negative form, Algiz describes vulnerability, danger, and forbidden acts, because this is a time when you are vulnerable. It can suggest that you may have to sacrifice something for no perceptible gain. There could be someone you should avoid or perhaps an offer that you should refuse. Someone may be using you, although it is possible that you are deceiving yourself or expecting something for nothing. It is advisable to be wary of new associations and also to avoid those who drain you or pull you down. Algiz can suggest a lack of contact with self-survival instincts and a lack of communication with your true nature. It can also warn about a period of sickness or the continuation of poor health. The message here is to look after yourself first, and only later to use your energies for the benefit of others.

Magical uses

In magic, Algiz is used to give protection from negative impulses and to fill a place with power. As an amulet it can be worn for protection.

Sixteen

SOWELO

The sound of "ss"

Origin

Sowelo is the sun rune and it is feminine in nature, as is the sun in Norse mythology and even in the modern German language. It is the counterforce to Isa. Sowelo is often connected to the lightening bolt, to a flash of inspiration, or to ecstasy. It strengthens spiritual and psychic powers and talents, and it provides enlightenment and success through individual will. It is a rune of understanding, education, and a transforming force that can represent high achievements, honor, and obtained goals. As a representation of the sun, Sowelo symbolizes that upon which all life depends. It is associated with the shining god, Baldur, the patron of innocence and light who is closely associated with mistletoe, a shaft of which was set into blind Hodur's hand by Loki in order to kill Baldur.

Positive interpretation

Sowelo represents a higher form of joy, happiness, and love. It is closely related to the heart and to the summer season. Sowelo symbolizes a strong positive force and life-giving warmth. Too little of it means lack of life and light, while too much sun brings drought and feelings of being burned out. Sowelo can resist death and disintegration and allow light to conquer dark. Its illumination allows you to see your goals more clearly. It promises good health, energy, clarity, optimism, confidence, and understanding. It is a rune of victory and success. It indicates a time when power is available to you for positive change in your life. In matters of love, Sowelo is a wonderful rune to find as it promises joy and happiness.

Negative or reversed interpretation

Sowelo cannot be read in a reversed position, but in its negative form it indicates a sudden change, sweeping things out of way, and possibly over-confidence or burnout. As a force, it can act as a weapon of destruction or it can clear away the old for the new. It can reveal your dark side—that side of your nature that is destructive to yourself and to others.

Magical uses

In magic, Sowelo is used to gain energy, healing and strength. As an amulet it can be worn to increase vitality.

Tyr's Aett

5

Tiwaz, Berkano,

Ehwaz, Mannaz,

Laguz, Inguz,

Othila, Dagaz

Seventeen

TIWAZ

The sound of "t" as in "ten"

Origin

Tiwaz is the rune of Tyr, the god of war, giver of victory and protector from harm. Wolfsbane, or "Tyr's helm," was used on arrowheads as a poison and was reputed to be a principal ingredient of witches' flying ointments. Tiwaz is also identified with the "spear rune" that an aging warrior supposedly cut into his own flesh so that he might enter Valhalla. It is commonly found on English cremation urns. Its meaning is primarily that of justice, as Tyr was the god that presided over the general assembly. Associated with the pole star, it represents guiding principles that are steadfast and that can be relied on when a traveler wishes to judge his position. In divination, it often refers to judgment, matters of law, decisions, or guidance. As Tyr's attribute is the sword, he represents unselfish courage and the warrior's energy. His clarity and wisdom can cut through the deepest darkness. Tiwaz brings the courage to enter dark realms, without knowing where or when or if you will come out into the light again. It gives an inner balance and it symbolizes potency.

Positive interpretation

Tiwaz is a rune of victory and success in any competition. It shows that you are ready to fight for what you believe in, and it promises success in battle. It denotes strong motivation and great strength and willpower. Tiwaz suggests the winning of disputes and the maintenance of law and order, therefore, it is a rune of stability, organization, and order. It indicates where your duties lie and it denotes self-sacrifice and responsibility. Dedication, bravery, objectivity, and authority are symbolized by this rune.

Tiwaz relates to binding oaths, and thus to commitment; while this is often taken to mean committing yourself to a cause or a fight, it can also relate to marriage vows (although nowadays, of course, this can mean a commitment that doesn't actually include vows taken in a church or county office). Tiwaz is an extremely masculine rune, so this suggests a marriage where the husband has the kind of strong and determined nature that makes the marriage hot and exciting. On the one hand, the sexual passions between the partners might run high, but with such a domineering man in charge, the woman will need to sacrifice some part of her own independence or identity. Battles might rage where two strong-minded people fight for supremacy, and jealousy and rage may never be far removed from the heat of sexual passion. Nevertheless, this is the kind of marriage that can stand the test of time and end up with two good friends entering old age together. In some castings, this can indicate a new romance, but if the reading is for a woman, she must weigh whether she wants to spend her life loving an exciting and difficult partner even before she gets into the situation.

Negative or reversed interpretation

In its negative form, Tiwaz may represent cowardice, weakness, and lack of initiative. It suggests defeatism, or perhaps conflict where there should be harmony. It may indicate a rigid nature of the kind that doesn't listen to others or to sense. It indicates failure in any context or competition that may be due to giving up too easily when difficulties occur, or as a result of acting in haste. If there is a question of romance, the man in the picture may not be honest, and he may also be selfish and irresponsible. Matters of trust and confidence are main issues but on some occasions this rune can refer to a relationship composed of short-lived lust.

Magical uses

In magic, Tiwaz is used to give strength, protection, and victory. As an amulet it can be worn for protection.

Eighteen

BERKANO

The sound of "b"

Origin

Berkano means "birch tree." This tree was regarded as sacred and it was associated with the fertility rites of springtime. Berkano is a feminine rune and is related to the earth goddess, so it represents manifestation and rebirth. In northern Europe, it is representative of physical beauty and attraction. It is strongly associated with Frigga in her maternal, caring aspect and thus represents all types of attractive female qualities. It also symbolizes nourishment, healing powers, and natural forces. Berkano is the rune of the earth, which receives the sacrifice or seed and then holds it within, guarding and nourishing it until the time has come for it to sprout and return again to the outside world.

Positive interpretation

Berkano represents birth or rebirth and it is also often referred to as the "birth rune." The birth in question might literally be the birth of a child, but it can also refer to the birth of an idea. Berkano is considered to be especially powerful in women's matters. It is concerned with the power of woman, with birth, and with regeneration. It can be thought of as the family rune, so it may refer to a happy family event. Being associated with motherhood, it can relate to one's own mother, but it is especially connected to the ideas of fertility and the care and nurture of infants and children.

Berkano represents new ideas, fresh starts, and a new projects—sometimes even a new romance—but whatever the new situation might be, it will be something that brings happiness.

Berkano symbolizes new growth, tenderness, and compassion. The new idea or project will need careful tending if it is to grow and develop, because if it is not properly attended to, it will, like a neglected child, die off. This rune is strongly connected with the family and home. It is also a rune of cooperation and perhaps a nicer and more peaceful atmosphere within a family. Berkano represents increased understanding and emotional stability. It hints at hidden transformation, awareness, and growth that may be attained after asking for spiritual help and guidance.

Negative or reversed interpretation

In its negative form, Berkano may represent infertility, and it can also indicate sickness for yourself or for someone around you who is sick and who needs to be cared for. It often indicates an unfortunate domestic situation that is fraught with arguments, and in the worst cases it can indicate too much sacrifice or martyrdom. Sometimes secrecy within a marriage or elsewhere, along with carelessness or loss of control, are among the negative aspects of Berkano. If you are deeply unhappy, this rune suggests that you ought to examine your own character in order to understand what is interfering with your own growth, or to discover what you are doing to draw such matters toward you. You may be putting your own desires above those of others, or you may be putting up with unreasonable behavior. Although a negative Berkano can indicate success, it is possible that this success won't be long lasting. In matters of business, the ventures that are involved will have trouble getting started or they may fall through. Business plans may need to be put aside until a later date.

Magical uses

In magic, Berkano is used to heighten fertility and help with women's problems. As an amulet it can be worn when wishing to make a fresh start.

Nineteen

EHWAZ

The sound of "e" as in "egg"

Origin

Ehwaz is associated with the twin gods or heroes, and also the divine twins or two horses. Ehwaz represents the harmonious relationship between two forces. It is closely connected to the "fetch," which is the horse that carries you on your journey between the two worlds, and with the eight-legged Sleipnir, the horse of Odin. Ehwaz facilitates the soul's travels or the shaman's journey, and it represents a journey in consciousness that is protected and guided. Horses have been regarded as sacred since the earliest times, and they were believed to be privy to the counsels of the gods. The horse was frequently regarded as sacred to Freyr.

Ehwaz is also a symbol of fertility.

Positive interpretation

Ehwaz's association with rapid progress and physical movement makes it representative of all forms of communication and travel; perhaps this includes your communications equipment, your vehicle, or your modes of transport. It can even be associated with hallucinogenics, which are used as a means of travelling between the two worlds. However, it is also associated with the natural changes that occur during life. Because it is attached to the ideas of movement and change, Ehwaz may indicate a change of occupation or a new address, although it often indicates a journey. You will soon be able to tackle problems in the right manner, which will bring a quick improvement and a new outlook on life. As long as your intentions are serious, your projects should flow smoothly from beginning to end and have a successful outcome.

Ehwaz symbolizes instinct, progress, trust, loyalty, and faith and it may indicate a partnership or marriage. It certainly signifies true friendship and fidelity.

Negative or reversed interpretation

In its negative form, Ehwaz shows that not all possibilities are open to you and you may be better off avoiding action or looking for new opportunities. On one hand, a lack of real direction may be a problem, while on the other hand hasty actions and reckless behavior will cause accidents. If you need medicines or medicinal drugs at this time, be especially careful that you do not overdose or use something that causes an adverse reaction. You may feel confined and restless and in need of a change, but it is best not to make decisions too quickly since it is too easy to waste time by taking the wrong direction. Problems may arise in connection with travel and transport, or it may be your ambitions that are being frustrated. Perhaps your loved ones are not in tune with your wishes and this may cause setbacks and frustrations. There may be health worries in connection with domestic animals or family pets.

Magical uses

In magic, Ehwaz is used to build power and bring people together or break them apart. As an amulet it may be worn to aid in communication.

Twenty

MANNAZ

The sound of "m"

Origin

Mannaz means "man," either as an individual or as part of human-kind, and in this sense it naturally also includes women. Mannaz is thought to offer powers for defense and protection. It is a rune of human existence and of the natural events of life and death, which makes it the rune of mortality. It also represents interdependence and support in addition to duty and responsibility. When cast, it may indicate the activities or situation concerning an individual or a group, or it can represent connections to others. It is a rune of assistance that suggests a need for help or a willingness to give aid to others. This rune represents our basic human qualities and our shared experience. It stands for the social order that supports the community and allows us to live in peace and to reach out and fulfill our potential. The qualities it emphasizes most strongly are those of being part of society, cooperation and support along with happiness. Mannaz is associated with Heimdal, the god who was raised by humans, and it is considered to be a rune of the mind rather than the emotions.

Positive interpretation

Mannaz contains two somewhat connected ideas: the first is your own status within your community or within your circle and the way that others perceive you; and the second is where you can go to look for help from others. As regards the first of these concepts, you need to assess your attitude toward others and also theirs toward you, and also to reflect on your own behavior before criticizing that of others. Thus, Mannaz suggests a time for personal reflection, and it is a rune of the rational mind, intelligence, structure, reason, and consciousness.

The second Mannaz concept represents a group effort or some form of pulling together, and it shows where you can expect to receive help or cooperation from others. The help you receive may be practical but it could equally come in the form of good advice. Mannaz can signify a good time for implementing plans and it speaks of constructive activity. It may show a new acquaintance who will enlarge your outlook and contacts. You must consider motives and behavior of others and consider the likely drawbacks of putting yourself under too much of an obligation to them. Nothing happens quickly when Mannaz turns up in a casting, so thought, consideration, and analysis of the facts will be needed before taking action. After you have taken time for this contemplation, you may have to wait for the group to shape up and pull the project together.

Negative or reversed interpretation

In its negative form, Mannaz can indicate that a problem has been blown up out of proportion, and it can also suggest that you are on the verge of giving up. At this point in time, you may need advice, but you will definitely need to maintain a positive attitude. The help you hoped for might not be forthcoming. You could be feeling isolated and lonely. In some cases, this may actually be a self-inflicted situation that has arisen out of a need to retreat from the world and to reflect on your life. Your self-esteem will be low, and you may lack the ability to communicate clearly with others. In some cases, there may be an enemy or an untrustworthy person around you. In yet other cases, Mannaz in its negative form can tell of a domineering father.

Magical uses

In magic, Mannaz is used to help social relationships and represent a particular person or group of people. As an amulet it can be worn to assist with reflection.

Twenty-one

LAGUZ

The sound of "l"

Origin

Laguz means "water." The Norse used the sea and rivers to move across continents and also for fishing, and so the sea and other bodies of water were considered a path to wealth and fertility. In addition, water was considered to be an expression of the unconscious and of the undiscovered mysteries of life and death. Like the water in a well, Laguz can bubble up from secret depths, but a lake can also reflect the view from above and therefore keep what is hidden under it a secret. Water seeks its own level and it takes the path of least resistance. Water is associated with death and the final journey. It holds all secrets and it represents the unknown. Laguz is associated with the Vanir god Njord, a wealthy deity who was associated with the sea. Seagulls and seals were sacred to him as were fjords, safe harbors, and inlets, and his personal emblem is the seashell.

Positive interpretation

Laguz symbolizes your emotions and intuition, your tears, and also your subconscious. It represents nudity, sensitivity, receptiveness, and vulnerability. It represents your ability to float along in the river of life and to adapt to circumstances with sensitivity. You will need to go with the flow or be washed away. Although you cannot live without water for long, you cannot live for long in it. Instinct and the depths of emotion are shown by Laguz . It shows your ability to empathize and to adapt to a situation. Your secret fears are revealed and encompassed in this rune. It advises you to use your intuition, to be aware of and alert to your feelings, and to find ways of fulfilling your emotional needs. Flexibility and adaptability are necessary. It suggests that sometimes you need to simply experience life without evaluating or understanding it.

In practical terms, Laguz can refer to the pleasurable aspects of life, to good fortune and success in trading, especially international trade or goods that are carried over water. It may mean that you have to wait for another party to make their moves before you can proceed with business, but it does indicate that success will come along. When this happens, you need to get moving and make the best of the opportunities that are on offer. Laguz can also denote good relationships and happy marriage and a safe emotional haven. Even when a relationship is going through a difficult patch, Laguz shows that it is basically a good one. Alternatively, if a relationship has ended, if you are lonely or sad, Laguz suggests that someone nicer will soon come along.

Negative or reversed interpretation

In its negative form, Laguz tells of the failure to draw on your instincts. You may be ignoring your inner voice, which warns against wrong actions or taking on things that are beyond your capabilities. Your fears may cause your emotions to be inhibited. You may suffer from depression or moods related to a desire to have something or someone who is not available to you, so a more flexible attitude will be needed. There is no point in cursing your fate or in drowning your sorrows in alcohol. This may be a time of confusion in your life during which you make wrong decisions and misjudge situations. There is a temptation to take the easy way out or to do something that is clearly wrong. There may be a woman in your life who will bring trouble.

Magical uses

In magic, Laguz is used to stabilize the emotions and intellect and to help in confronting fears. As an amulet it can be worn to give strength and enhance your psychic abilities.

Twenty-two

INGUZ

The sound of "ng" as in "thing"

Origin

Ing is the horse-god of fertility. Other symbols for this sign are the boar, the cuckoo, the apple and laurel trees. Ing is considered to be a doorway to the astral plane. In Germanic languages, "ing" can mean son of, as in "atheling" or son of the king, and it even turns up in science fiction books as earthling, meaning someone from earth as opposed to some other part of the galaxy. There is a possibility that Ing was an actual human who belonged to the nation known as the eastern Danes. Ing is certainly associated with Denmark, and by extension with Britain after much of it was taken over and run by the Danes and unified under King Canute (King Knut).

The Norse god of fertility, Freya, is associated with Inguz. It can be a rune of horses, although Freya preferred to ride a wild boar named Gullinbursti ("golden bristles"), and the bristles on the animal's back were said to symbolize golden wheat.

Positive interpretation

Inguz is associated with the start of a new season or phase, the beginning of a new project, and of fertility and growth. It indicates health and well-being and also a fertile mind that is full of good ideas, as well as the energy and motivation to make a start on a new project. Sometimes, it is necessary to see off an old project before making a fresh start, so Inguz can indicate that loose ends need to be tied up, jobs completed, and the decks cleared in readiness for the next phase. Even if there is no indication of a new phase at this point in time, Inguz tells you that it is just around the corner, so it is well to clear the way for it.

Sometimes Inguz literally means clearing out cupboards, the attic, or clearing barns, offices, or even the car in readiness for something new. Sometimes Inguz can indicate inheritance, and probably the need to clear out somebody else's house and perhaps to keep some part of its contents for yourself. In other circumstances, Inguz indicates a time to get rid of those people who pull you down, who use you for their own ends, or who may hinder your progress or your ability to make a fresh start. Inguz can suggest that you take a break or a holiday in order to step back from your situation to allow yourself to take a different perspective.

Negative or reversed interpretation

Inguz cannot be read in a reversed position, but if surrounded by negative runes, it warns that fear, indecision, or laziness may cause you to miss opportunities. It also suggests that you consider whether the words and behavior of others is designed to hold you back or keep you from making necessary changes. It may suit their interests for you to remain stuck in a situation that is not doing you much good. Whatever the situation, courage and faith in the protection of your spiritual guides will help you to break free and to make the fresh start that you need.

Magical uses

In magic, Inguz represents gestation; it brings fertility and growth, and restores balance. It is used as a talisman to encourage good health and for the protection of the home.

Twenty-three

OTHILA

The sound of "o" as in "old"

Origin

Othila means "inheritance" in the sense of anything of value that can be handed down or passed on, and this includes knowledge. Othila encompasses the customs and attitudes of the ancestors as well as the inheritance of property, material things, or physical attributes. It represents the wise management of family assets. It also represents loyalty, duty, and the responsibilities that go along with maintaining family ties.

Othila is associated with land, so it represents cultivation in all its aspects. This may imply actual crops, or some form of creativity through culture, art, and craftsmanship. Othila can represent the growth of the intellect and emotions. It is concerned with establishing and making your mark on history. It is also representative of your ancestors and of any previous lifetimes that you may have experienced. Othila is often associated with Odin, the father of the gods. It resists arbitrary rules and seeks to preserve individual and collective liberty within the framework of natural law. Like a family secret, Othila is something to be carefully guarded and watched over.

Positive interpretation

Othila refers to possessions, land, the home, and those items that you already own or that you will acquire, which means that it can also relate to inheritance. However, it is just as likely to tell of inherited talent, behavior, or characteristics. Othila may refer to religious, group, or family traditions that have become hallowed and which are comforting, especially in times of stress. This rune refers to family history, group loyalty, and to your roots. It can relate to patriotism, love of country, an interest in history (either history in general or family history), a religious group, or the clan, tribe or dynasty to which you belong. It can mean becoming part of a group of like-minded people that make you feel safe and useful. Othila can indicate help from older people or old friends. It symbolizes the values of your family and culture.

Othila may indicate that you are living in a closed world and that you need to open up more, or that you are too tied to the family, the clan, or the past. Thus it suggests freedom and independence through releasing ideas and even releasing yourself from those things that keep you stuck.

Negative or reversed interpretation

In its negative form, Othila indicates that you may be bound by old conditioning and are refusing to let go of outmoded ideas and concepts. Sometimes this means overturning the established order of things and bringing chaos to the family or group. Perhaps you need to consider what benefits you and others. Othila can refer to a lack of roots or of isolation. Sometimes it indicates delay and frustration. It can indicate disputes over money, goods, and inheritance and legal problems related to land and property; so where Othila is concerned, it is important to be patient and pay attention to detail. It can warn against trickery or theft. In modern terms, a negative Othila can refer to problems with vehicles or machinery. You may lose some of your possessions, possibly due to trying to move too fast. Success is possible but this is further away than you would like it to be.

Magical uses

In magic, Othila represents land, property, and ownership. As an amulet it can be worn to bring wisdom and power to you from all sources.

Twenty-four

DAGAZ

The sound of "d"

Origin

Dagaz means "day." This contained a period of both dark and light as the Norse counted their days from evening to evening with the midpoint at dawn. Sometimes Dagaz relates to the hours of daylight, and specifically to noon. It is often associated with Thor, the god of lightning who brings inspiration, so it represents transformation and awakening, and the passage from darkness to light. Dagaz can represent paradox and the balancing of opposites as complements rather than as contradictions. Dagaz is a rune of clear vision and enlightenment and it represents time and space. It is the rune of polarization and of good fortune. The coming of daylight offers security and a time when you can see your foes coming and so counteract them. Fears and phobias can also be countered at this time.

Positive interpretation

Dagaz is a wonderful rune to find if your life has been in limbo or if you have not been making progress, for it suggests that a time of waiting will soon be over and that major events and turning points are on the way. It is a rune of good fortune. Dagaz refers to a time when work can successfully go ahead. As one of the runes that is identical when reversed, its independence is further enhanced, because no matter how life turns out, its energy cannot be turned or reversed and its transformation is always positive. Dagaz may signify protection when new people or situations enter your life. Dagaz has great protective powers and is a rune of health, prosperity, and new openings. It can prevent harm and encourage helpful energies. It is a rune of change, of gradual but slow improvement, prosperity, and completion. It represents the end of an era and the beginning of a new day. Occasionally, Dagaz can bring secrets out into the open or it can show why a particular route or activity has been blocked or closed to you. This revelation allows you to move forward with the kind of clear vision you have when the sun is shining rather than continuing to grope in the dark.

Sometimes Dagaz is associated with children and it indicates that any children in your circle will be happy and successful. It can also indicate fun and happiness, new and pleasurable activities, and a burst of fresh energy.

Negative or reversed interpretation

As a rune of increase and growth, Dagaz has no negative aspects, so even when surrounded by difficult runes it shows an inner strength that can be used in times of difficulty. It counteracts delay and shows slow and steady progress. It brings the end of an era and the dawning of a new day full of hope and optimism. It can indicate a major change for the better. At worst, it can show that you are drawing problems to yourself by dwelling on them too much.

Magical uses

In magic, Dagaz can be used to invoke an awakening of the senses. As an amulet it can be used for protection and it is often used for the protection of entrance-ways.

The Blank Rune

WYRD

Origin

In some traditions, Wyrd is said to be the mother of the Norns and the one who wove the web of fate that covered the then known world. Therefore, Wyrd can be viewed as the force that judges both gods and mortals and rewards or punishes them for their actions. It can also be considered to be the rune that cuts short their mortality.

Interpretation

In a reading, the blank rune of Wyrd means fate, destiny, kismet, or circumstances and events that are beyond our control. Those of us who live in the modern world find it hard to believe in fate or karma because we prefer to think that our own free will can override destiny. Accidents happen, people fall in love or come home and find that their spouse has walked out, people even win things or lose them. Life is not always in our hands; sometimes it is just a matter of destiny. All we can do is live through both good and evil times and learn from them.

"The Norns," from *Die Helden und Götter des Nordens, oder Das Buch der sagen.*
G. Gropius, 1832

Reading
Runes

6

Before you even begin a reading for another person, you need to put your client at ease and assure him or her that you are reliable and trustworthy. You must inspire confidence by being able to recognize, name, and describe the meanings of runes without referring to books. In addition, you must remember that this is the client's reading and it should address his or her needs. Advice offered by the runes can be frank and may not always be what the client wishes to hear. You should offer your interpretation as diplomatically as you can, but also guard against the tendency to "sugar coat" the message; in this case the meaning becomes lost.

Attitude

Even if you are doing a reading for practice only, you should still take your reading seriously and think carefully about the way you word your information. Some people may claim they don't believe in the runes, but what you say will still have an effect on them. The best way to present yourself is to imagine how you would feel in the client's position. It is all too easy to inflict unintended emotional damage, and you won't want your clients to leave feeling worse than when they arrived!

Rune reading is tiring so it isn't a good idea to undertake a reading when you are feeling less than your best. People can be demanding, and some will ask you to give them a reading no matter how bad you feel or how late the hour. Few matters are so urgent that they cannot wait a short time. When someone is in distress, it can be very difficult to stand back from them, but it may be necessary for the preservation of your own mental health.

What you are aiming to do is to offer information, reassurance, and grounds for hope, but if a client is in desperate straits, unless you are a trained and skilled counselor, there is a limit to what you can do.

Tolerance is essential for any reader. You may have views completely different from your client on any number of matters, but the reading is for them and it is only their views that matter. You also owe your client complete confidentiality. If you want to discuss your reading with another practitioner, you should seek permission from your client and then make sure that his or her identity isn't revealed.

There is nothing wrong with accepting payment for your work. Interpretation of the runes is a skill requiring study and practice, and just like anyone else providing a service, you are entitled to payment. It is best to set a rate for the job when making the initial appointment.

Preparation

Although any surface can be used for your runes, many people prefer to have a special cloth, and some like to have separate cloths for each spread, with the spreads labeled on them. Additionally, many rune casters like to put symbols of the different elements on the table with them. A candle may be used for fire, a bowl of water for water, a feather for air, and a crystal or stone for earth. These symbols can be purely decorative or used in your reading by passing the runes over each in turn before laying them out. Earth is usually placed to the north, air to the east, fire to the south, and water to the west.

Before you begin a reading you should wash you hands. Not only will this help to protect your runes but it will also show respect to them. Your washing can be turned into a ritual act of purification. While washing away the dirt on your hands, you can visualize your fears and doubts being washed away.

You may wish to ask your spiritual guide or deity for help with the reading and also ask your guide to offer good advice and to give spiritual healing to your client during the course of the reading.

Casting the Runes

Reading the runes is referred to as "rune casting." This term applies whether you are throwing the runes, or placing them by hand into a spread. If you are casting (throwing) the runes out rather than laying them out in a spread, you will need to select a rune that embodies the question to stand as the significator of the question. Don't take the rune out of the bag; leave all the runes in place but jot down the name of the rune or make a mental note of it. If the client's question refers to a matter of business or money, choose a rune that represents this, or if the questioner wishes to know about a health matter, select an appropriate rune. If the significator rune shows up in the reading, things are unlikely to change.

A question about love, life, and happiness belongs to Freya's Aett so the significator rune should be chosen from that Aett.

If the question concerns intellect, understanding, and spiritual growth, it belongs to Hagal's Aett. If the question is about daily life, work, house moves, family problems, and so forth, it belongs to Tyr's Aett.

It is natural to want to read each rune in isolation but if you do so you are likely to miss out on a whole level of information. The runes in a spread interact with each other. Sometimes two runes have very similar meanings, and this emphasizes the importance of the message.

Some runes act as "power" runes, dominating those around them and modifying the tone of surrounding runes. Those that relate to gods or start one of the Aettir demand such attention. These are Fehu, Ansuz, Thurisaz, Hagalaz, Tiwaz, and Mannaz. The presence of one or more of these runes in a spread shows that the gods are taking a particular interest in the situation. Wunjo can moderate the tone of surrounding runes, and while it cannot change the meaning of any runes nearby, it may reduce any problems indicated by other runes.

Throwing the Runes

The simplest method of casting the runes is to pour the runes onto the floor or table and then interpret each rune that lands facing upward. If a rune falls upside down or rests on its side, you should ignore it. If a rune falls on its side between two runes, read it to see what is linking the other two runes. When choosing the runes to read in this way, you need to look over your cast carefully to decide which runes are close to one another.

If you require a defined area, take a cloth and draw two circles, one inside the other, on the cloth. The inner circle represents the past, the outer circle the present, and the area outside both circles represents the future. Alternatively, the runes in the innermost circle may represent the heart of the question, while those further out might represent environmental or other factors.

Another method is to point the top of your cloth toward the north and then to consider any runes that fall in this direction to represent some kind of difficulty, while those that fall toward the south can be seen as useful and helpful, even if they are difficult in nature. Runes that fall to the east represent things that are known, or events arising out of the past, while those that fall to the west indicate events that have yet to be revealed. When you consider the geography of northern lands, the north is a hard place, the south is where the light and warmth come from, the east was the land that was known, and the west was unknown .

If you decide to read the runes in the open air, you can use a piece of chalk or a stick to draw a circle on the ground. Stand in the circle and focus on the question, gently throwing the runes and taking note of where they land. The closer they are to you, the more significant they are to the question. You also take note of how close they fall to the person who is asking the question, to the other runes, and to the circle itself.

When you have fixed the question in your mind and thrown your runes, allow your intuition to take over. Look for any patterns in the way the runes fall. If the shape reminds you of something then allow this to guide you. For example, if the pattern reminds you of a boat or an airplane, a journey could be indicated. If the pattern reminds you of a the shape of a specific rune symbol, that particular rune will be relevant to your question, even if it isn't included in pattern itself. Start by reading the runes that are nearest to you and then continue by working outward, away from yourself.

If you wish to use reversed meanings, ensure that you turn the runes over from left to right or right to left, moving them horizontally rather than vertically, so that you don't reverse an upright rune, or vice versa.

Other Suggestions

- The runes that fall in the center of your cloth can be used to represent the predominant issues of the question, while those that are away from the center can be considered outside the main issue.

- You can use the inner runes as the heart of the matter and the outer ones for surrounding circumstances.

- See how many runes land face down, as these can show hidden elements that are behind the scenes.

- The more runes that land upright, the more positive the reading.

- Runes that touch or cover other runes are closely working together in some way.

- Areas on the cloth can represent the past, and others can point the way to the future.

Rune
Spreads

7

There are several choices when it comes to finding suitable spreads for rune reading. You may find a particular spread that you feel comfortable with and stick to that one, or you may wish to use a variety of spreads. It is probably best to begin with something simple, because it can be confusing for a beginner to deal with too many runes at once. As you gain more experience, you can use more complex spreads that will provide more information.

Before making your decision about which spread to use, you must consider the client and his or her requirements, the issue in question, and how you yourself feel at the time of the reading. If you don't feel like laying out a host of runes and you consider that a simple spread will offer sufficient information, then go with your feeling.

When your questioner has a decision to make, a spread of one to three runes is ideal. A larger number of runes is useful when a fuller picture is needed.

When you are using spreads rather than simply throwing the runes, the method is to choose the runes from the bag, place them face down in the spread formation on the cloth or surface you are using, and then turn them over horizontally, always from left to right.

Single Rune Spread

Drawing a single rune is the simplest method. It does not enable you to look at a situation in detail but it can provide a quick answer or it can help you or your questioner to make a decision. Clear your mind and think of your question and then pull one rune from your bag. Consult the meaning of this rune and see how it applies to the question. If you wish to use this for yourself, you can take one rune every morning to show you the sort of day to expect.

One rune can be used in this way to answer a specific "yes or no" type of question. In this case, if the rune you have pulled from the bag is oriented in the upright position, the answer is yes. Runes that cannot be reversed should always be considered to be upright.

Three-Rune Spreads

Spreads that use three runes are extremely popular. They are easy to use and they offer a reasonable amount of information. There are many different three-rune spreads but here are two useful ones:

Reading one

Position 1: The problem or issue at hand

Position 2: The best course of action

Position 3: The likely outcome if the advice of the runes
is taken

Reading two

Position 1: The questioner's present physical condition

Position 2: The questioner's present mental condition

Position 3: The questioner's present spiritual condition

The Four Dwarves Spread

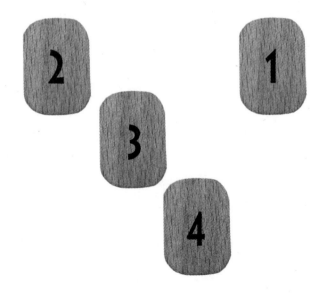

Here are two ways of reading this spread:

Reading one

Position 1: Past wishes in relation to the question

Position 2: Present wishes and how the questioner feels about the situation

Position 3: The wishes and feelings of others and how they affect the situation

Position 4: The questioner's heart's desire that he or she keeps hidden from the world

Reading two

Position 1: The basic influences that surround the question

Position 2: Problems and obstacles that may affect the outcome

Position 3: Positive influences at work

Position 4: The immediate outcome

The Cross of Thor

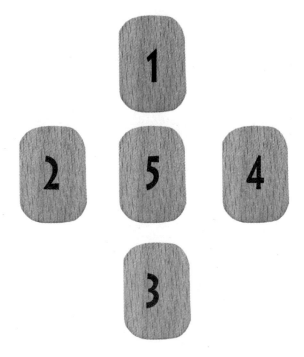

In this spread, two of the runes perform a predictive function, so this is particularly good for matters of money and business.

Reading

Position 1: The situation

Position 2: The obstacles

Position 3: Supportive forces

Position 4: The short-term outcome

Position 5: The long-term outcome

The Runic Cross spread

This layout can be used in two different ways.

Reading one

Position 1: The past

Position 2: The present state of mind

Position 3: The possible future

Position 4: The basic influences underlying the question

Position 5: Events and factors that will help or hinder a
successful outcome

Position 6: The most likely outcome

Reading two

This is particularly useful for a questioner who wants to know about
his or her career, and it is sometimes called the "career mirror."

Position 1: The questioner's current position

Position 2: The challenge being faced by him

Position 3: The questioner's greatest strength and ability

Position 4: The questioner's past experience with regard to
the matter at hand

Position 5: The questioner's future plans—and their
usefulness or otherwise

Position 6: The future outcome

The Seven Worlds Spread

The reading

Position 1: The things that fate is throwing at the questioner

Position 2: Things working in the questioner's favor; also expansion, growth, fertility, and pleasure

Position 3: Force and strength, though a difficult rune can suggest weakness

Position 4: The core of the question and the questioner him- or herself

Position 5: The questioner's skill, purpose, and ability

Position 6: Dangers and forces opposing the questioner, also the effects of greed, anger, and fear

Position 7: Hidden factors and things that aren't as they seem

The Combined Runes Spread

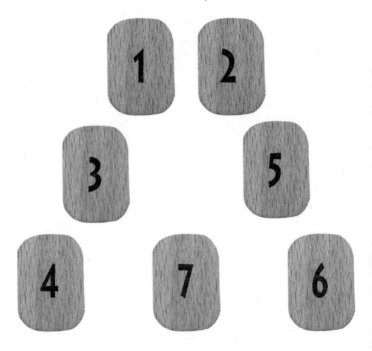

This spread involves reading the runes in pairs.

Positions 1 and 2:   The issue or problem

Positions 3 and 4:   How the past influences the current situation

Positions 5 and 6:   The advice the runes are offering

Position 7:   The outcome of the situation if the
questioner follows the advice that is given

The Mimir's Head Spread

The runes in this spread are read in pairs.

Positions 1 and 2:   The issue at hand.

Positions 3 and 4:   The reasons for the problem.

Positions 5 and 6:   Solutions and ways of resolution.

Position 7:   The result and final outcome.

The Grid of Nine Spread

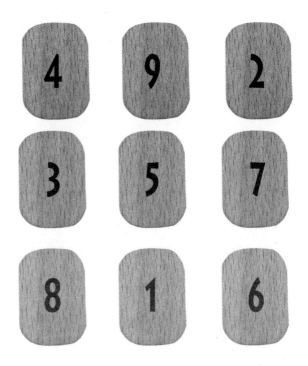

This formation is an ancient symbol also known as the Magic Square of Saturn. The position numbers of the lines add up to fifteen and the The position numbers in the whole square total 45.

The bottom row represents the past.

Position 8: Influences from the past

Position 1: The basic past influences

Position 6: The questioner's attitude to those past events

The middle row represents the present.

Position 3: The hidden influences that are operating at the time of the reading,

Position 5: The current state of affairs

Position 7: The questioner's attitude toward the present influences

The top row represents the future.

Position 4: The hidden obstacles, delays and problems that can affect a successful outcome

Position 9: The best possible outcome

Position 2: The questioner's response to the outcome.

The Cosmic Axis

RUNES PLAIN AND SIMPLE

Position 1: The major past influences that bear upon the
                     questioner

Position 2: The unconscious response to the major past
                     influence

Position 3: The conscious response to the major past
                     influence

Position 4: The results of the influences that have led to the
                     present state of affairs

Position 5: The present

Position 6: The current unconscious responses

Position 7: The current conscious responses

Position 8: What happens if the questioner does nothing to
                     alter the flow of energies

Position 9: The major outcome of the question at hand

Position 10: The unconscious response to the outcome

Position 11: The conscious response to the outcome

The Four Quarters of the Year Spread

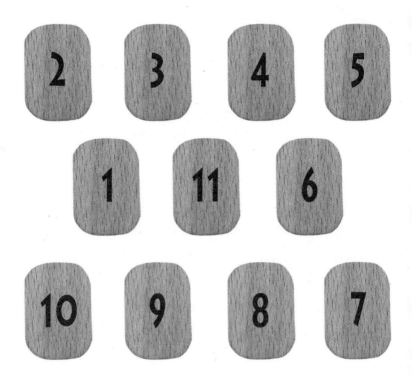

This spread is used when you need a precise answer to a complex question. This spread also gives an overall view of life for the past six months and the coming six months

Positions 1, 2, and 10:	The first quarter; the questioner's present state of mind
Positions 5, 6, and 7:	The second quarter; helpful or opposing influences in regard to the question
Positions 3 and 4:	The third quarter; what will happen if things continue in their current direction
Positions 8 and 9:	The fourth quarter; possible outcome of the question six months from now
Position 11:	The overall tone of the spread.

Rune Magic

8

The primary use of runes is for divination, but runes can also be used for magic. Rune magic is field of study separate from rune divination, so what follows is a very brief overview. To achieve any success in rune magic you need to develop a deep understanding and familiarity with mythology and history of the runes.

In the ancient Northern magic tradition there were essentially two different strands of magical practice. Seidhr was shamanistic in nature and it involved trances, dreams, and astral travel to and through the nine worlds. Like many ancient forms of magic, Seidhr could have a darker side that was intended to bring sickness and even death to one's enemies. Galdr was closer in nature to ceremonial magic. It involved the use of talismans and charms, particularly those that are spoken aloud. Most rune magic is of this sort.

The Eights

There are eight different techniques that are involved in rune magic. The number eight has great significance with respect to the runes, as reflected by the three Aettir: there are eight runes in each Aett.

1. The first stage is selecting the right material, which is to be used for magical runes.

2. The second technique relates to cutting or marking of the rune glyphs. Making a rune was a precise process that involved cutting into the material to be used, and the cuts had to be in a made in a specific order if the runes were to

be used for magic. When runes are made for this purpose the rune caster needs to be aware of the meaning of the runes and be sure that what is being cut is appropriate.

3. In the third stage, the cut runes are then stained; there are a number of references about staining the runes with blood if they are to be used for magic. Modern rune casters suggest that this is purely symbolic and that red paint can be used instead. However, many purists consider that the use of blood to be an important part of the process.

4. The fourth stage is that of testing, and this means not only evaluating the rune to be used but also a testing of the rune caster him- or herself.

5. The fifth stage is that of evoking or asking. This is a spoken command that transforms the glyphs from carved characters to activated runes.

6. The sixth stage is the stage of blessing the runes, performing a ritual to dedicate them to a specific god, and preparing them for use.

7. The seventh stage is that of sending. This is a technique that focuses the magical power of the runes and sends it toward the target of the spell.

8. Finally, during the eighth stage, the rune caster feeds the rune with his or her strength and energy.

Names as Charms

The use of individual runes as charms is well established in both archaeology and in the literature of northern Europe. The magical meaning of the runes is closely related to their divinatory meanings—for example Fehu is used magically to attract wealth, although it could also be used negatively to deprive another of material comfort. Positive magic with runes is known as "weal working," whereas negative magic is known as "woe working." Both the positive and negative forms of magic were used in the past. However, the majority of charms were defensive and protective. For example, instead of trying to kill an enemy, a charm would be used to make sure that the enemy's attacks had no effect. There are several references to charms being activated with spoken commands that were said to trigger them. The exact runes used for charms as described in the "Havamal" magical text is open to debate.

Bind Runes

Bind runes are runes that are combined to increase their magical power. Two or more runes are inscribed onto each other to form a new pattern, and this is then used as a personal symbol or worn as a pendant. There are two main types of bind rune: those made from a person's name or initials, and those made from specific runes to combine their qualities.

It is quite popular to construct a bind rune using runes that make up the initials of your own name, but these may not actually be runes you may want to be closely associated with. The second method involves combining runes according to the result that you are looking for. For example, if you need courage and strength combined with resilience and good judgment, you would combine the runes Uruz and Tiwaz. Wearing this as a pendant would enable you to draw these properties into your being.

When making a bind rune, the two that are chosen for the purpose need to be combined in a way that is pleasing to the eye and that has a kind of symmetry. Choosing suitable runes for the effect you require takes serious thought, but that is only the first stage. If you choose the wrong runes you will still have a result, but it may not be the one you had hoped for. Another way in which rune magic may be worked is to carve a suitable rune three times on a talisman or candle, as this is represents completion on all three planes. Traditionally, the magical energies are classified into three parts: the elements, the runes, and the gods. In combining the runes, each of these is addressed. Other symbols besides runes were used in Old Norse magic. Some of these symbols were variations on the runes, and others simply referred to a single concept or deity, such as the hammer of Thor.

To make a talisman you need to carve or paint the rune onto an item and carry it accompanied by a suitable herb or crystal. The tables on the following pages shows the magical correspondences for each rune. Table 1 shows the corresponding gods, colors, stones, and trees. Table 2 shows the corresponding flower, herb, astrological sign or planet, and card of the Tarot.

Table 1: Magical Correspondences: Gods, Colors, Stones, and Trees

The Rune	The God	The Colour	The Stone	The Tree
Fehu	Aesir	Light red	Moss agate	Elder
Uruz	Vanir	Dark green	Carbuncle	Birch
Thurisaz	Thor	Bright red	Sapphire	Hawthorn
Ansuz	Odin	Dark blue	Emerald	Ash
Raido	Foresti	Bright red	Chrysoprase	Oak
Kaunaz	Freya/Dwarves	Light red	Bloodstone	Pine
Gebo	Odin/Freya	Deep blue	Opal	Elm
Wunjo	Freyr/Elves	Yellow	Diamond	Ash
Hagalaz	Ymir	Light blue	Onyx	Yew
Nauthiz	Normir/Etins	Black	Lapis lazuli	Rowan
Isa	Rime/Thursur	Black	Cat's eye	Alder
Jera	Freyr	Light blue	Carnelian	Oak
Eihwaz	Idhunna/Ullr	Dark blue	Topaz	Yew
Pertho	Nornir	Black	Aquamarine	Aspen
Algiz	Valkyrjur	Gold	Amethyst	Yew
Sowelo	Sol	White/silver	Ruby	Juniper
Tiwaz	Tyr/Mani	Bright red	Coral	Oak
Berkano	Frigg/Nerthus/Hel	Dark green	Moonstone	Birch
Ehwaz	Freya/Freyr Aclis	White	Iceland spar	Holly
Mannaz	Heimdal/Odin	Deep red	Garnet	Ash
Laguz	Nhord/Baldr	Deep green	Pearl	Willow
Inguz	Ing/Freyr	Yellow	Amber	Apple
Othila	Odin/Thor	Deep yellow	Ruby	Hawthorn
Dagaz	Odin/Ostara	Light blue	Crysolite	Spruce

Table 2: Magical Correspondences: Flowers, Herbs, Astrology, and Tarot

The Rune	The Flower	The Herb	Astrology	The Tarot
Fehu	Lily of the valley	Nettle	Aries	The Tower
Uruz	Nasturtium	Sphagnum moss	Taurus	The High Priestess
Thurisaz	Honesty	Houseleek	Mars	The Emperor
Ansuz	Morning glory	Fly agaric	Venus	Death
Raido	Snapdragon	Mugwort	Sagittarius	The Hierophant
Kaunaz	Gorse flower	Cowslip	Venus	The Chariot
Gebo	Wormwood	Heartsease	Pisces	The Lovers
Wunjo	Larkspur	Flax	Leo	Strength
Hagalaz	Fern	Lily of the valley	Aquarius	The World
Nauthiz	Crocus	Bistort	Capricorn	The Devil
Isa	Sweet pea	Henbane	The Moon	The Hermit
Jera	Cornflower	Rosemary	The Sun	The Fool
Eihwaz	Lilac	Mandrake	Scorpio	The Hanged Man
Pertho	Chrysanthemum	Aconite	Saturn	Wheel of Fortune
Algiz	Sedge	Angelica	Cancer	The Moon
Sowelo	St. John's wort	Mistletoe	The Sun	The Sun
Tiwaz	Red hot poker	Sage	Libra	Justice
Berkano	Moonflower	Lady's mantle	Virgo	The Empress
Algiz	Forsythia	Ragwort	Gemini	The Lovers
Mannaz	Foxglove	Madder	Jupiter	The Magician
Laguz	Water lily	Leek	The Moon	The Star
Inguz	Gentian	Selfheal	New Moon	Judgment
Othila	Snowdrop	Clover	Full Moon	The Moon
Dagaz	Pot marigold	Clary	Half Moon	Temperance

Initials

If you like the idea of using your initial as a talisman or engraved on something and threaded through a leather cord as a pendant, the following table will show the corresponding rune to the letter of our modern alphabet. However, take care that your initial suits your requirements and that it is not a difficult or unlucky rune. If your initials are SS you may decide against this method of making a talisman. Similarly, if your name begins with an H, you might conjure up the destructive power of Hagalaz; if your name begins with an I or EE sound, as in names like Eve or Yvonne, you will be drawing the frozen and immobile power of Isa.

Bear in mind that the English alphabet equivalents are phonetic: Ansuz may look like an "F" in our alphabet, but its sound is that of "a."

English	Rune	Futhark	Pronunciation
A	Ansuz	ᚠ	As in Annie
B	Berkano	ᛒ	As in Barry
C	Sowelo	ᛋ	As in Cindy
C	Kaunaz	ᚲ	As in Cathy
D	Dagaz	ᛞ	As is David
E	Ehwaz	ᛗ	As in Evan
E	Isa	ᛁ	As in Eva
E	Eihwaz	ᛈ	As in Eileen
F	Fehu	ᚠ	As in Fannie

G	Gebo	X	As is Gary
H	Hagalaz	N	As in Hannah
I	Isa	I	As in Isobel
I	Eihwaz	ʃ	As in Ivan
J	Jera	⟨	As in Jay
K	Kaunaz	⟨	As in Karen
L	Laguz	⌐	As in Larry
M	Mannaz	M	As in Mary
N	Nauthiz	⨸	As in Nadia
O	Othila	⨂	As in Oscar
P	Pertho	K	As in Paula
Q	Kaunaz	⟨	As in Quinn
R	Raido	R	As in Ralph
S	Sowelo	⟨	As in Sylvia
T	Tiwaz	↑	As in Tammy
U	Uruz	∩	As in Oona
V	Fehu	⊬	As in Victor
W	Wunjo	P	As in Walter
X	Algiz	Y	As in Xavier
Y	Isa or Jera	I ⟨	As in Yvonne
Z	Algiz	Y	As in Zarah
Ng	Inguz	◇	As in Ingrid
Ng	Inguz	◇	As in Nguyen
Th	Thurisaz	▷	As in Theodore

Runic Calendar and Clock

You may like to check out the calendar to see which runes rule the various weeks of the year. Each rune rules two weeks, so in this way you can check out the rune for your date of birth or for any date in any year. For example, if you have something special planned for a particular day or week (like a wedding!), you may like to see what the runes have to say about this. In addition, each hour of the day is ruled by a rune, so if you have a special time planned for some event or for a meeting, see what the runes have to tell you.

It is interesting to note that Hagalaz covers Halloween—and some say that the name "Halloween" derives from a form of the word "Hagal" or "Hagalaz."

Table of Dates and Hours

Dates	Runes	Hours
29 June to 14 July	Fehu	12:30 pm to 1:30 pm
14 to 29 July	Uruz	1:30 pm to 2:30 pm
29 July to 14 August	Thurisaz	2:30 pm to 3:30 pm
14 to 29 August	Ansuz	3:30 pm to 4:30 pm
29 August to 13 September	Raido	4:30 pm to 5:30 pm
13 to 18 September	Kaunaz	5:30 pm to 6:30 pm
28 September to 13 October	Gebo	6:30 pm to 7:30 pm
13 to 28 October	Wunjo	7:30 pm to 8:30 pm
28 October to 13 November	Hagalaz	8:30 pm to 9:30 pm
13 to 28 November	Nauthiz	9:30 pm to 10:30 pm
28 November to 13 December	Isa	10:30 pm to 11:30 pm
13 to 28 December	Jera	11:30 pm to 12:30 am
28 December to 13 January	Eihwaz	12:30 am to 01:30 am
13 to 28 January	Pertho	01:30 am to 02:30 am
28 January to 12 February	Algiz	02:30 am to 03:30 am
12 to 27 February	Sowelo	03:30 am to 04:30 am
27 February to 14 March	Tiwaz	04:30 am to 05:30 am
14 to 30 March	Berkano	05:30 am to 06:30 am
30 March to 14 April	Ehwaz	06:30 am to 07:30 am
14 to 29 April	Mannaz	07:30 am to 08:30 am
29 April to 14 May	Laguz	08:30 am to 09:30 am
14 to 29 May	Inguz	09:30 am to 10:30 am
29 May to 14 June	Othila	10:30 am to 11:30 am
14 to 29 June	Dagaz	11:30 am to 12:30 am

Try another practical guide in the
ORION PLAIN AND SIMPLE
series

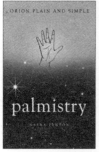

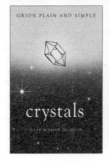

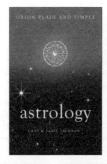

ORION PLAIN AND SIMPLE

astrology
CASS & JANIE JACKSON

totem animals
CELIA M. GUNN

runes
KIM FARNELL

palmistry
SASHA FENTON

body reading
SASHA FENTON

numerology
ANNE CHRISTIE

chinese astrology
JONATHAN DEE

crystals
CASS & JANIE JACKSON

reincarnation
KRYS & JASS GOULY

angels
BELINDA GRASHAWAY